THIS SPREADING TREE

The Story of The Leprosy Mission
from 1918 to 1970

1974
———

The Leprosy Mission
50 Portland Place
London W1N 3DG

Copyright © 1974 by The Leprosy Mission. First printed in Great Britain 1974. ISBN 0 902731 12 2. All rights reserved. No part of this publication may be reproduced or transmitted in any form or by any means, electronic or mechanical, including photocopy, recording, or any information storage or retrieval system, without permission in writing from the publisher. This book is sold subject to the condition that it shall not, by way of trade or otherwise, be lent, re-sold, hired out or otherwise circulated without the publisher's prior consent in any form of binding or cover and without a similar condition including this condition being imposed on the subsequent purchaser. Printed in Great Britain for The Leprosy Mission, 50 Portland Place, London W1N 3DG by Lawrence-Allen Ltd., London and Weston-super-Mare. Tel. 0934 21415.

Contents

Foreword 5

PART ONE: THE TREE GATHERS STRENGTH
            (1918-1934)
Chapter 1: View from a Dublin Window 8
Chapter 2: After Paul, Apollos 10
Chapter 3: Root and Branch 15
Chapter 4: The New Treatment 25
Chapter 5: Jubilee 36

PART TWO: THE TREE WITHSTANDS THE
            STORM (1935-1945)
Chapter 6: The Lull Before 52
Chapter 7: The Storm Breaks 67

PART THREE: THE SPREADING TREE
            (1945-1960)
Chapter 8: How the Tree began to Spread ... 84
Chapter 9: On Tour 100
Chapter 10: In Conference 118

PART FOUR: WIDER AND WIDER YET
            (1960-1970)
Chapter 11: Five Fruitful Years 132
Chapter 12: Consultations 151
Chapter 13: The Near North 162
Chapter 14: General Council 183

Foreword

SIR HARRY GREENFIELD, C.S.I., C.I.E.
(Chairman of the Council of The Leprosy Mission)

THE LEPROSY MISSION continues to make history; and it will assuredly go on doing so for many years to come.

It would be premature therefore at this stage to attempt a definitive History of the Mission. Yet the unfolding story should be made known, for it is an epic of so many human virtues: of courage and imaginative enterprise; of endurance and resourcefulness; of fidelity to ideals; of patience in the face of frustrations and disappointments; of unfailing loving-kindness; and of much else besides.

The high qualities shown by men and women who have served the Mission down the years, and by those to whom they have ministered, should be enabled constantly to shine before men, so that they may find appreciation and perhaps emulation; and the celebration of the Centenary seems a specially appropriate occasion to look back down the road travelled by our predecessors and by those who are proud to follow in their footsteps.

The story of the early years has been admirably told by our beloved Donald Miller in *An Inn called Welcome*. The present volume takes up the narrative from the year 1917. It has been compiled from a mass of varied documentary material which has accumulated in the Mission's archives during a span of fifty-three years.

The title of the book draws upon the parallel of the banyan tree—a tree held sacred by many in India where the Mission's work first began, and which is capable in its most luxuriant form (as in the Botanical Gardens at Calcutta) of sheltering hundreds of people. The metaphor is aptly chosen, both because the Mission has afforded shelter to many in sore need; and because the natural habit of the banyan tree, as it grows in stature, is to put out roots from its branches and the Mission has likewise taken root in many countries.

The narrative is simply told, for the very good reason that

the facts narrated speak for themselves. They tell of a continually growing campaign, conscientiously and faithfully pursued by men and women of many lands seeking their own answers to the question "Who is my neighbour?".

As with so much else in the Mission the production of the book has been assisted by several devoted hands, to whom we must all be grateful. The one who has borne the main burden prefers to remain anonymous, but his name will surely be inscribed in the great Book of Memory as one who walked humbly in the steps of his Master and was a most faithful servant of the Mission.

The record they offer to us is one of proud service, a service which commands general thanksgiving and which must continue, because the challenge offered by leprosy throughout the world has yet to be overcome.

Part One

**THE TREE GATHERS STRENGTH
(1918 - 1934)**

Chapter One
VIEW FROM A DUBLIN WINDOW

THE 1914-1918 WAR was grinding remorselessly on. Great armies were still locked in the rain-sodden trenches and ruined landscapes of the various Fronts, particularly the Western Front. The warring nations were still pouring out their treasure and their blood in a conflict that never seemed likely to end. Dermot Harvey Bailey, the youngest son of the founder of The Leprosy Mission, had been killed in action in May 1917, and in this year of 1918 the Minutes of the Committee record resolutions of sympathy with friends of the Mission who had suffered a like grievous loss. There must have been many more who had paid a heavy price in anxiety and sorrow as they daily scanned those long lists of the killed, the wounded, and the missing. And still the agony went on. In February of 1918 there must have been very few who could see the breakthrough that would shortly come, and still fewer who would have dared to prophesy that the war would end in November of that year. So it was that on a February afternoon in 1918 the view from the window of 20 Lincoln Place, Dublin, was dark indeed.

It was there that a meeting of the Committee of The Mission to Lepers in India and the East, as it was then called, took place. Mr. G. W. Place, LL.B., was in the chair; seven members of the Committee were present, with the General Secretary, Mr. W. H. P. Anderson, in attendance; four members sent apologies for absence. Such is the modest beginning of the second part of the history of The Leprosy Mission. The Minutes, neatly written by hand, put on record the first formal acts of the Committee after the retirement of the Founder.

On June 18th, 1917, the office of the Mission had been opened at this address by Mr. Wellesley C. Bailey—almost the last public occasion on which Wellesley spoke before he retired at the age of 71. The office of the Mission's Committee for Ireland is still at the same address.

This was the Committee's one hundred and fifty-seventh meeting. If, instead of looking out at the bleak prospect we have just described, the Committee had looked back, there would have been many reasons for encouragement and thanksgiving. Under the leadership of Wellesley Bailey the Mission had grown slowly but steadily in the manner described so vividly by Donald Miller in his book, *An Inn called Welcome,* which covers the Mission's story from the first meeting in Monkstown, Dublin, to the retirement of the founder in 1917. The Spreading Tree was small compared with what it was to become, but it was firmly planted and had begun to grow vigorously.

In the Minutes of that particular meeting there is no indication of either looking out or looking back in the sense we have just mentioned. The Committee applied itself to the business in hand. There is indeed one indirect reference to the War: Mr. William Hayward was granted an annual allowance 'while he is on service with the Forces'. Otherwise the Committee attended strictly to business. It does not seem very important now, but it was important then, and the Committee took it seriously.

At this point we may well pay tribute to Committee and Council members who in many countries through many years have done just that. They have seldom made headlines, but patiently and steadily they have applied their hearts and minds to the work, and the growing strength of the Mission is a testimony to their faithfulness through the years. They are the unnamed stalwarts of this enterprise, 'my other fellow-workers whose names are in the book of life' (Phil. iv, 3). And we add to them the great host of supporters of this work whose faith and prayers and gifts have given vitality to the Spreading Tree.

What then was the view from that Dublin window on that February afternoon in 1918? Whatever the Committee may have thought of the Western Front, or of past achievements, they were aware of the challenging and beckoning vista that opens up on those 'greater works' that Jesus said His disciples would be privileged to do for Him (John xiv, 12).

Chapter Two
AFTER PAUL, APOLLOS

IN SUCCESSION TO Paul the apostle, God called to Ephesus an Alexandrine Jew named Apollos, a man with a different background, a different outlook, and a different method. There are diversities of gifts, but if there is the same Spirit God uses the talents of one man to complement those of another. So it was at an important point in the history of the Mission. After Wellesley Bailey the pioneer, W. H. P. Anderson the consolidator. Certainly they were very different men, just as Paul and Apollos were. Bailey was an Irishman, Anderson a Canadian. Bailey might fairly be described as a gifted amateur, while Anderson belonged to the professional class. But both were dedicated men, and God blessed both. 'I planted the seed,' says Paul, 'and Apollos watered it; but God made it grow' (I Cor. iii, 6, NEB).

William Henry Penny Anderson was born in Guelph, Ontario, Canada, on the 27th June, 1874, the year in which the Mission was founded, of Scottish-English parents, who were members of the local Presbyterian Church. After a conventional education he studied accountancy and was admitted a member of the Ontario Institute of Chartered Accountants at the age of twenty-six. Two years later he crossed the border and spent three years in the United States on the staff of a Boston firm of accountants.

As a young man of eighteen, William Anderson had been in the audience when Wellesley Bailey, on his first visit to Canada, spoke about the Mission at the home of a Mrs. Watt, who founded the Mission's auxiliary in Anderson's home town of Guelph, Ontario. Now here again in Boston he heard the Mission's story at a meeting addressed by John Jackson, the Deputation Secretary of the Mission, who was on tour in America at the time. The seed sown by Wellesley Bailey years before now bore fruit.

The very day after Mr. Jackson's lecture William Anderson made a definite offer of service. It was explained to him that it was not the policy of the Mission to appoint missionaries. If therefore he really desired 'to do something for lepers'—to quote his own words—his best course of action would be to join a missionary society already engaged in leprosy work. This he did the following year.

Giving up a promising future in his profession William Anderson joined the American Evangelical Mission, and was appointed to Chandkhuri in the Central Provinces of India. He at once began work in the leprosy colony; only three months after his arrival in India in October 1905 he took over the superintendency of the institution and served it faithfully for seven years. Here his ability for business organization found full scope and there were many signs of progress at Chandkhuri. But the central point of his ministry was always a concern for the individual sufferer. In due course William Anderson was appointed to be the Mission's Secretary for India and so gained wider experience of the work which he was soon called upon to lead as General Secretary of the Mission.

Evidence of this concern for the individual is not hard to find. Mr. and Mrs. Anderson produced a little book called *Mending and Making*. It is undated, like most of the early publications of the Mission, and is apparently based on Anderson's experience as superintendent of Chandkhuri and as Secretary for India. The book contains several stories about individual patients, such as Aeneas:

Aeneas was of the cultivator caste and lived in South India. His mother and a younger brother were lepers. At the age of 17 he noticed patches on his body where the skin had become lighter in colour. His marriage had been arranged, but as he believed himself to be leprous he decided not to be married. Certain of his village people now prevailed on his parents to ask him to leave his home, which he did. He went first to one of the great places of pilgrimage. Here he fell ill and was befriended by a Christian teacher. The leprosy now began to develop rapidly and ulcers appeared. For the past fourteen years Aeneas has been an inmate of one of the larger asylums of the Mission. When he first came he was quite illiterate, but he soon learned to read and write, and in turn taught the leper children in the Home. He became a fine Christian character and the chief Elder. The other leper men hold him in much respect and his decision in any dispute is accepted without protest. As Aeneas can neither stand nor walk, a roughly made four-wheeled cart has been provided for him in which he is drawn about the Asylum or to the Church. He attends the services in the latter regularly and takes a special joy in speaking about his Saviour to non-Christian lepers.

Then there is another story about a clever girl patient, and how old Elizabeth ministered to her:

Eight years ago a young girl was brought to one of the Homes in the Central Provinces—another promising student from a Christian school. Her friends thought a bright future lay before her. She had a natural aptitude for teaching, knew English in addition to three Indian languages, and was clever with her fingers. Then—and how often is the sad story repeated—it was discovered that she had in some way contracted leprosy. So they brought her to the Home, a young girl with crushed hopes, almost stunned with the shock. A veritable messenger of God is sometimes disguised in the crippled body of some poor leper. Such an one was old Elizabeth, many years a leper, but uncomplaining and with a bright spirit unconquered by suffering. She it was who took the lonely, bewildered girl to her heart, mothered her and sweetened as far as she could for her the bitter cup. That was eight years ago, and— today? There is today in that Home a young woman whose dark eyes are haunted with wistful sadness, but who greets you with quiet dignity and a welcoming smile. The leper children gather naturally about her; she teaches them and is their friend, in school and out of it. The influence of her Christ-like life is felt throughout the institution and the missionaries turn to her for help as they turned in days gone by to Elizabeth, now gone to her rest.

W. H. P. Anderson had a quiet sense of humour, shared by his wife, and there were times when laughter was possible among the sufferers:

The visitors had nearly finished their tour of a leper home in Mid-India. They had talked with men, women and children, had seen the school and dispensary, and the chapel already too small for its needs, when they came upon a dilapidated erection near the women's quarters, quite out of keeping with its neat surroundings. 'What is this?' they asked, curiously surveying the gipsy-like tent of rough matting. The group of leper folk following them were seized with such convulsions of laughter that no coherent answer could be given at first. Then an old dame, shaking with merriment, explained that this rough shelter was really a house of correction. When any woman became refractory and quarrelsome, disturbing the peace and comfort of others, she was banished to the hut by those who shared the same room. This apparently had a tranquilizing effect and after a night or two the delinquent—now in a repentant state of mind—was glad to return to her corner of the Home.

William Anderson was appointed General Secretary of the Mission in succession to Wellesley Bailey in 1917. By the time this second part of the history of the Mission opens in 1918 Anderson was already established in Dublin and fully engaged in the task to which he was to give so many years of fruitful service.

It must soon have become clear to Mr. Anderson's acute mind that, attractive as Dublin was, it was not the best centre for an organization now firmly established and actually approaching its Golden Jubilee. It was not on the main sea routes west to the U.S.A. and Canada or east to India, China and Korea, and it was becoming increasingly clear that the chief executive officer of the Mission must be more suitably located. (On one occasion Anderson was delayed for eighteen days through missing a boat connection between Dublin, London, and New York.) More important still from the General Secretary's point of view, London was not only the heart of the Empire, but was also the place where many Missionary Societies had their headquarters, and to establish the head office of the Mission at this centre would greatly facilitate that co-operation with these Societies which was one of the Mission's main objects of policy.

The exact reason for the move is not given either in the Minutes of the Committee or in the brief notification in the Mission magazine. However, the Committee did in fact decide that Dublin should become the headquarters of the Committee for Ireland, which it still is, and the head office of the Mission should move to London.

Another major decision in which Mr. Anderson must have played a leading part was even more important. This was the decision to re-constitute the Committee of the Mission as a Council, with wider membership and a formal constitution.

The Constitution now drafted by the Dublin Committee provided the Mission with an amended title, 'The Mission to Lepers', without reference to India or the East, and so opened the way to future wider fields of service. The aim of the Mission was defined in the same general terms as at present, except that the term 'lepers' in the text of the document was later amended to 'sufferers from leprosy', and it is noteworthy that even at that date the Mission looked forward to the eradication of leprosy from the world. The main impression is that of the remarkable far-sightedness of its author or authors, for it stood for many years with only minor amendment until its revision more than forty years later. A striking example of this foresight not mentioned in the above provisions was the power to establish an International Committee, a power which lay latent for many years until it was invoked at the time when the Council began to plan the Lucknow Conference of 1953.

On May 17th, 1921, the Dublin Committee met for the one hundred and seventy-fifth and last time as the Committee for the Mission as a whole. Two days later at a special Meeting for Members in London the new Constitution was adopted and the Council appointed. On the last day of the same month this new Council met for the first time, elected Sir William Fry, D.L., as its Chairman, formally accepted responsibility for the management of the Mission's affairs, and proceeded at once with the business before it. Apart from the name of Sir William Fry the list of Council members included familiar names—Dr. Thomas Cochrane, the Hon.

Mrs. Arthur Gordon (elected in place of her late husband), Sir Walter Kinnear, and Mr. Walter B. Sloan, while at the next meeting of the Council in June two more names appear, those of Sir Edward Gait and Sir Leonard Rogers.

When we think of the great changes which have taken place in the world since the Council first met in 1921, we cannot but be deeply impressed by the faith, the courage, and the wisdom of those who under God shaped so fine and strong an instrument for the furtherance of His will in Christ in this ministry to the suffering.

Chapter Three
ROOT AND BRANCH

WHAT IS THE source from which the Spreading Tree has drawn its strength? As Wellesley Bailey put it:

> The Mission has been born and cradled in prayer; it has been brought up on prayer; it has been nourished on prayer; and prayer has been at the bottom of its success from its first moments of life.

It is still true that the Mission is 'brought up on prayer'. Every meeting held by the Mission, whether a Council or Committee meeting for the transaction of business, or a public meeting for the advocacy of the cause, begins with prayer and usually ends with further prayer. At many centres regular prayer meetings are held. The working day at the head office of the Mission in London begins with staff prayers, and no doubt this is the general practice at the Mission's offices in all other centres. Add to this the great volume of private prayer offered by friends of the Mission in various parts of the world, aided in recent years by the Prayer Manual entitled *Daily Remembrance*. Consider also the prayers offered in many languages by the staff and patients in the Mission's Homes and Hospitals. The list is an impressive one, and the most impressive thing about it is that this chain of prayer has gone on and on, unbroken through the long years of the Mission's history.

Even so, has prayer been literally the basis of the Mission's achievements through all this time? One naturally hesitates to question the memorable words of its distinguished founder, but it does seem as if the root of the Spreading Tree goes down further still. Prayer is itself the expression of a more fundamental spiritual experience, in this case a sense of deep compassion for the suffering and of total commitment to do all that can be done for their relief. Even more basic is the example of the Lord Jesus Himself and the command which He gave to His disciples to 'cleanse the lepers', to which the loving heart responds in joyful obedience. This does not claim to be a precise definition of the motive underlying all that the Mission does, but it does point to that hidden spring of spiritual power and refreshing grace from which the Spreading Tree draws its life. Year after year, and indeed generation after generation, it has produced a wonderful response in prayer, in service, and in gifts.

Now a tree is an organism—that is to say, a body with connected independent parts sharing a common life, to quote one dictionary—and it must organize these independent parts to the fulfilment of its purpose. So we come to the various auxiliaries, the roots of the Spreading Tree, which draw from a deep well of spiritual experience this outflow of dedicated gifts of money and personal service, and channel them through the trunk to the areas of need.

At the time when this second part of the Mission's history opens there were three offices of the Mission in Great Britain. One was at 20, Lincoln Place, Dublin, as we have seen; another in Scotland at 28, North Bridge; and the third at 33, Henrietta Street, Covent Garden, London, to which the head office of the Mission moved in 1921. The Secretary in Dublin was Thomas A. Bailey, while in the Edinburgh office Miss E. McKerchar had been established as Secretary for Scotland since 1917 and was to continue to give the Mission faithful service for many years. In London a change was made following the death of John Jackson; C. Douglas Green was appointed Secretary for England, and William Hayward, now returned from service with the Forces, became Editorial Secretary. The Minutes of the Committee for 1918 also contain a brief reference to the North of Ireland and the first mention of T. W. Wynne, who was given a small allowance for office expenses and apparently used a room in his house as his office. In 1920 he was appointed Honorary Secretary for Belfast and District with formal recognition of the 'Belfast Auxiliary' as it is called in the Minutes.

1924 was a year of significance as well-loved pioneers moved on; Mrs. Wellesley Bailey and Miss Jane Pim to their eternal reward, and Thomas Bailey to retirement.

As pressure of work increased, the premises at 33 Henrietta Street became too small, and a move was made to 7 Bloomsbury Square, where the Council met for the first time on October 7th, 1930.

In 1918 support was being received in varying amounts from established Auxiliaries in Canada, Australia, New Zealand, India, Switzerland, and the United States of America. The most progressive of these Auxiliaries was undoubtedly the American Committee, as it was called.

Its fund-raising efforts were so successful according to the standards of the time that after a visit to New York in 1919 Mr. Anderson went so far as to say, 'It is only a matter of time till the largest part of the home income will be derived from the United States.'

On the other hand there was nothing to indicate any tendency to seek control of the work on the field. 'There seems to be complete confidence in our administration of the work abroad, together with a full recognition of our desire to carry out reasonable and necessary extension'. At this time and for years later relations between London and New York were extremely cordial, and in this happy situation no doubt Mr. Anderson himself played an important part. The fact that he had worked for three years in that accountant's office in Boston was perhaps a help to him in appreciating the American point of view. Certainly a warm welcome was given to Mr. William Danner, the General Secretary in New York, and to Dr. William Jay Schieffelin, the Chairman of the American Board (whose name was later given to the Leprosy Research Sanatorium at Karigiri), when they visited London.

We have said above that several Overseas Auxiliaries were already active by 1918, but this does not mean that they had been established in a formal sense. They represented the spontaneous response of Christian love, and for years continued to contribute to the Mission's funds. But soon it became necessary to strengthen the links between these Auxiliaries and the Council of the Mission and thus give a greater measure of unity to the parts of the Spreading Tree. Accordingly in 1925 constitutional proposals were made for Ireland, Canada, and Australia. William Anderson the consolidator was thus complementing the work of Wellesley Bailey the pioneer.

In the meantime matters had taken a different course on the other side of the Atlantic. On June 14th, 1920, the American Committee had taken action designed to strengthen the Committee's appeal in the United States. This was the formal incorporation of the American branch of the Mission as a separate Society known as The American Mission to Lepers Incorporated, with its own President and Board of Directors administering its own funds. It did not become a property-holding body, and properties of the Mission on the field remained vested in the Leper Mission Trust Association. The new Society accepted responsibility for Homes superintended by American missionaries in certain areas, and for such Homes in India an agreed proportion of costs was accepted in what came to be known as the co-operative budget. This arrangement has continued to the present time, though with some modification, and has been a lasting outworking of the close co-operation between the Council in London and the Board in New York. The American Mission to Lepers, Inc. (later known as American Leprosy Missions, Inc.) thus ceased to be an auxiliary of the parent Society and established itself as an independent legal entity, though remaining a co-worker with The Mission to Lepers and sharing through the years the burden of the campaign against leprosy.

The Indian Auxiliary was the first example of an Auxiliary formed in a country where leprosy is prevalent. In 1918 William Anderson received a long letter from the Chairman of the Indian Auxiliary proposing that the Indian Auxiliary Committee should be given executive powers, and asking, if so, to what extent? In the long history of the Mission different answers have been given in different circumstances; in 1918 the answer was to approve the establishment of an Auxiliary Committee for India, but as an advisory body without power to deal directly with the superintendents of the Homes who were missionaries representing co-operating Societies. Similarly, these missionary superintendents would be under no obligation to report to the India Committee; they would continue to work under the Secretary for India and the Home Committee in Dublin, as was the practice when Wellesley Bailey directed the work.

When the General Secretary visited India in 1920 he met members of the Indian Auxiliary and discussed with them arrangements for the re-organization of the Auxiliary on a new basis. A formal constitution was proposed, including a more representative membership, and with the approval of the Auxiliary itself this was put to the Council and adopted two years later in 1922. In the meantime Anderson drew the attention of the Home Committee to the fact that its own constitution did not provide for the organization of National Overseas Committees and Auxiliaries, an important hiatus that had to be closed if the parts of the Spreading Tree were to hold together in unity with the Central Council. This matter had attention when the new Constitution of the Mission was adopted, as we have already seen, and the power to form Auxiliaries and National Committees was specifically given to the new Council. The record of this change in the Indian Auxiliary therefore marks a definite stage in the development of the Mission as an organized Society.

It provides a convenient bridge to the next part of our subject—the out-reach of the Spreading Tree as typified by its branches. The organization of the work on the field did not require as much revision as that of the Auxiliaries. For many years the system inaugurated by the founder of the Mission continued to work satisfactorily. This was a system of close co-operation with Missionary Societies engaged in leprosy work by providing their personnel with facilities enabling them to carry it on. The advantage to the co-operating Societies was that they could continue to engage in this work at little or no extra cost to themselves, while the advantage to The Mission to Lepers was that it did not have to bear the heavy cost of training and equipping missionaries and supporting them on the field.

So for a good many years the Mission appointed no missionaries of its own, with one notable exception mentioned below, and was therefore able to use its funds in other ways, particularly in response to new requests for help in leprosy work which continued to come in from time to time. This may sound rather a loose connection with the co-operating Societies and their representatives, but in practice it was stronger than might have been supposed. Indeed old files suggest that for at least some of the major institutions correspondence with London was so detailed that it is sometimes hard to say who was really the superintendent of the Home in question—the missionary on the field or the General Secretary in his London office.

Another means of drawing together the work in a given area was by the appointment of Field Secretaries such as the Secretary for India, whose duty was to visit the Homes, to encourage staff and patients, to discuss problems on the spot, and to report to the Council on the needs of the work. There were also occasions when he was able to give a valuable second opinion on a scheme put forward by some enthusiastic Superintendent.

At the time of the opening of this part of the Mission's history this appointment was held by the Rev. Frank Oldrieve, a Baptist missionary who had worked at Subathu. He was officially appointed Secretary for India, with effect from January 1st, 1918, but held this office for only a short time. In 1923 he withdrew from the Mission on acceptance of the Secretaryship of the newly formed British Empire Leprosy Relief Association with the goodwill of the Council and thanks for his services. In the meantime a similar arrangement had been made for the supervision of the work in China and Korea by the appointment of a Secretary for Eastern Asia.

The aim and object of these administrative arrangements was never lost sight of—the battle against leprosy. Those involved often had direct responsibilities for some sector of the front. Thus the Secretary for Eastern Asia, Dr. Henry Fowler, was Hon. Superintendent of the Leper Asylum at Siao-Kan in Central China. From this Home Mrs. Fowler reported the following:

> Some years ago, one morning in spring, little Wan La T'ing came to the Siao-Kan Leper Home. I am quite sure that when he was born he was welcomed to his home as all boys are in China, and for a few years he was the joy of his mother's heart. But his health began to fail, he was taken to a hospital in Hankow, and there the doctor said he was a leper. His uncle realised how dangerous the disease was in the family, and urged that La T'ing should go to a Leper Home. So, one day, Mrs. Wan came bringing her little son. He was a bright, happy little lad, and did not seem to realize what it all meant. Naturally Mrs. Wan wanted to see where her little boy was to live, so we all walked over together to the Leper Home. La T'ing slipped his hand into mine and did not seem a bit afraid. We were glad that there was such a pretty, clean, comfortable place to show Mrs. Wan. She was very quiet and brave as we walked round the buildings and garden, and saw everything; but the end came. She pulled out some cash to give

the little lad, and as she was talking to him the head nurse (himself a leper) said to La T'ing 'Come with me, I have something to show you' and off went the boy happily. The nurse did not want the little chap to see his mother leave. While he was away she left, and very likely has not seen him since. He was not suffering then, for the disease was not far advanced, and he settled down very quickly and happily. We hope that with the new treatment he may be cured. We have just visited the Leper Home for Christmas, and La T'ing is looking well. He has learned to read and to write, and asked me to send him some picture story books. He has already joined the Church and been baptized on confession of faith.

The third element in the co-ordination of the work on the field was provided by visits made by the General Secretary in person. William Anderson went to the field to study the work at first hand in India and Burma in 1920, in India, China, and Korea in 1925, and in Korea, China, Japan, and Formosa in 1932. During the 1932 tour Anderson attended the Shanghai Leprosy Conference, the first such conference ever held in China and noteworthy as being convened under the auspices of The Chinese Mission to Lepers.

We have mentioned already that at this time it was not the policy of the Mission to appoint missionaries. In 1920, however, while Anderson was on tour in India, he heard of a proposal of the Bengal Government to take vigorous action in the segregation of pauper lepers by the establishment of a large settlement on the lines of a farm colony to house about a thousand persons of this type. Mr. Anderson told the Council that if the Mission were actually invited to manage this settlement it would be a great opportunity for the extension of the Mission's work in Bengal, though it would mean sending out a man from home to give his whole time to this piece of work. When, the following year, a candidate presented himself the Council was reconciled to this new departure and accepted the offer of service made by this young man, fortunately for him at the time and even more fortunately for the Mission in later years. His name was A. Donald Miller, and in due course he went out to Purulia to learn Bengali and prepare himself for his expected task. As it turned out this particular scheme came to nothing and Donald Miller was not called upon to manage the proposed new colony. Instead he was appointed Acting Secretary for India on the withdrawal of the Rev. Frank Oldrieve—the right man available at the right time. That was in 1923, and only two years later he was confirmed in this appointment as Secretary for India.

In maintaining a balance between resources and needs the Council must have had some anxious moments. At the end of the Minutes for 1918 the estimates of expenditure for the following year are given in detail. They total £37,030—a large enough sum at that time. It was in fact an act of faith in the continuing goodness of God and the generosity of His people, and it was justified by the event. The money came and the work went on. Even so we note a certain nervousness in magazine articles about the Mission's finances in those early days. A steady flow of reports and stories from needy areas showed just how worthwhile it all was.

Some years later, the Secretary was on tour in India and had already visited a number of Homes. Wherever he had gone he had been given what might be called V.I.P. treatment. There had been garlands galore, gay decorations, welcome meetings, songs and dances, special functions of several kinds, and at Champa, where he arrived at night, a torchlight procession to lead him in triumph to the Church building. But of course he knew very well that these tributes were intended to express the joy and gratitude of the patients to the Mission and its supporters, not to him personally. If he had any remaining doubt about this, he was soon put right. He had completed his inspection of one of the Homes in Central India and had just complimented the women patients on the beautiful decorations with which they adorned their houses, when a group of the older women settled down for a chat. As the visitor was still within his language area there was no need of an interpreter, and a lively conversation followed:

The old lady who had elected herself spokeswoman for the group did not ask my name; she knew it already. But she did go on to ask me some of the usual questions, not because she was inquisitive but because this was a village woman's idea of showing a polite interest in the visitor. Was I married? How many children had I? Much shaking of heads at my reply. Was I employed by the Mission? Where did I work for the Mission? So it was true that I had come from England? How far had I travelled? I explained that I had not only come from England to India but had also already visited a number of the India Homes, so the total distance I had travelled to date must be about seven thousand miles. 'It sounds a long way', she said vaguely. I do not think she understood a distance like that, so far outside her limited experience. After a moment's pause for thought the next question came. 'Did you pay your fare?' I was not particularly surprised by this question. When India became independent the simple village people of India thought that the railways belonged to them, and they could travel free. The railway authorities had a lot of trouble with passengers who had no ticket. 'Yes,' I replied, 'the fare was paid'. 'How much was it?' I did a little mental arithmetic and then gave her a round figure. 'About three thousand rupees (£225 sterling).' She gasped, and the other members of the group stared open-mouthed at this astonishing figure. She did not understand seven thousand miles, but she certainly understood three thousand rupees—a small fortune to her. 'Do you mean to say that you paid three thousand rupees out of your own pocket?' 'No', I said, 'I did not pay; the Mission paid for me.' 'But *somebody* paid?' 'Yes,' I said. There was a pause while they all digested this surprising fact. Then the old lady took a deep breath, gave her nearest neighbour a violent nudge with her elbow, and said with a broad grin, 'Did you hear that? Three thousand rupees to come to see us. We must be Very Big People!'

Well, that was one way of putting it! The V.I.P. is not the visitor, however distinguished he or she may be. The Very Important Person is the patient.

Chapter Four
THE NEW TREATMENT

IN OCTOBER 1925 William Anderson reported to the Council on the long tour which he and his wife had just completed. From the written account of this tour one sentence stands out:

There is general agreement that we should drop the use of the word 'asylum' in describing the institutions of the Mission.

In order to appreciate the significance of this remark it will be worth while to make a list of the various names given to these institutions through the years. The list throws light on one aspect of the history of the Mission, and enables us to date with some accuracy an important change of direction in Mission policy. This is the list of names, all taken from official records:-

(a) Asylum
(b) Leper Home
(c) Leper Home and Hospital
(d) Leper Hospital and Home
(e) Leprosy Hospital
(f) Sanatorium

Nowadays the word 'asylum' has for many people a rather unpleasant connotation which it did not have when Wellesley Bailey began to use the word. Then it meant just what it said. The institution was a refuge for the needy and the distressed, a sheltered haven where loving care was given to those rejected and often scorned by society at large. The 'Home' was an extension of the asylum idea, an attempt to create a kind of life in which the people concerned could engage in various activtites as far as their disabilities allowed, and thus build up for themselves a community spirit which would compensate them to some extent for the loss of contact with the world outside. The addition of the words 'and Hospital' marks the beginning of the real fight against leprosy as a disease, and when instead of 'Home and Hospital' we have 'Hospital and Home' we see clearly the growing importance attached to medical work, emphasized still further when the institution becomes a 'Leprosy Hospital' or even a 'Sanatorium'—that is to say, a place where the patient will go for a course of treatment to make him fit to return to the outside world. This list carries us far beyond the Diamond Jubilee of 1934 which ends the period now under review, and we shall return to this subject later.

What we now notice is the significance of the change from (b) to (c), when 'Leper Home' becomes 'Leper Home and Hospital'. It indicates a major step in a new direction, and there is no doubt when this occurred. In the Council Minutes of 1925, the year in which William Anderson suggested that the word 'asylum' be dropped, approval was reported as given to a scheme for a new institution at Foochow in China; and this propsed institution was to be neither an 'Asylum' nor a 'Leper Home'; it was formally described as a 'new Leper Home *and Hospital*', the very first use of the word in the Minutes of the Council.

What was it that showed the new way the Mission was to take? The answer lies in what was called 'The New Treatment', which we have already seen mentioned in Mrs. Fowler's story about La T'ing.

This treatment was new in the sense that it was new to the work of the Mission. For some years previously investigations had been carried on by a number of leprosy workers who had turned their attention to the old herbal remedies known in India and China, and now began to take seriously the question of oil therapy. As a result of tests made at Culion, in the Philippines, one of the research workers, Dr. Heiser, suggested to Sir Leonard Rogers that a full-scale investigation should be made into an old remedy, the oil of the seeds of the chaulmoogra tree. This was undertaken at the School of Tropical Medicine in Calcutta, of which Sir Leonard Rogers was in charge at the time, and included both detailed laboratory tests and extensive field trials.

Dr Ernest Muir, who had already had the opportunity of observing the frustration of leprosy workers in Mission institutions, now joined in the search for an effective method of using chaulmoogra, or alternatively oil derived from the seeds of other trees of related species which might be more readily available than chaulmoogra oil. So we come to hear of hydnocarpus oil, made from the seeds of *Hydnocarpus wightiana*, a tree which grew in South India. Impurities caused distress to patients so further research was directed to purification of this oil and its manufacture in India on a large scale and at a reasonable price. In this way the traditional remedy was modernised and made widely available as the standard treatment for leprosy.

Word of the new treatment spread rapidly and brought fresh hope to sufferers from leprosy and to those working among them. For so long their work had been frustrated by the knowledge that, however devoted their ministry was, it seemed to produce no direct result in the medical field. Now at last there appeared light at the end of a long and dark tunnel. There was 'hope for the leper', and the 47th Annual Report of the Mission actually carried the title 'Hope Abounding'.

As a sample of the enthusiasm with which the new treatment was greeted, here is an extract from a report by the then Secretary for India, the Rev. Frank Oldrieve:

> During the last few months I have visited all the large leper asylums in India, and wherever I have gone there is a different spirit among lepers. And I do not marvel. Their ulcers are being healed; their faces, so marred, are becoming normal again; sensation is returning to the places where there had been anaesthesia, and strength is coming back. The present treatment is a hypodermic injection of the ethyl esters of hydnocarpus oil, and the latest preparation gives no troublesome reaction. Lepers are now eager to take the injection and even little children do not dread it.

It may be doubted whether some of Mr. Oldrieve's remarks should be taken quite literally. Was sensation really returning to places where there had been anaesthesia? Did the little children face those injections without dread? It is true that in India there has always been great faith in the *sui*, the needle, because it seems to put strong medicine in the very spot where it is most needed, but it must also be said that the process of injection was unpleasant and while it was generally heroically endured there were wry grimaces and even tears sometimes.

Side by side with Oldrieve's testimony we set the words of Dr. Muir, who is described in the 1922 magazine as 'Leprosy Research Worker, School of Tropical Medicine, Calcutta':

> We are finding that with this treatment even advanced cases of leprosy make wonderfully rapid progress towards recovery, and that large numbers lose all signs of the disease. We do not, of course, make any extravagant claims. We do not, for instance, hope that many of the deformities which have been incurred will be remedied. Fingers which have been lost do not grow on again; noses that have been flattened will remain so unless reshaped by operation. Neither do we ensure that there will not be a recurrence of the disease in those who have lost all signs of it.
>
> A few *lepra bacilli* may remain hidden somewhere in the body and these may find an opportunity to light up again when the body has, for some reason or other, been reduced to below par. For the above reasons we refuse to use the word 'cure', a word which we consider inapplicable to leprosy.

So at this early stage of the oil therapy programme Dr. Muir was hopeful but his optimism was tinged with characteristic caution. On the other hand an experienced missionary doctor of the American Presbyterian Mission in Korea, Dr. Fletcher, did not hesitate to use the word 'cured' in this story of the successful use of oil therapy, and its striking sequel when the patient returned to his village:

> Our city of Taiku is but seventy-seven miles from the most southern port, Fusan. Seventy-five miles to the east of us, on the coast of the Sea of Japan, is a little village which has recently become of special interest to us. Three years ago the villagers had a mass meeting and decided to inform Oh Sung Goo's parents that they must leave the place or

compel their son to leave. Their reason was fear of contamination for the village well, due to the fact that Oh Sung Goo was a leper. The parents knew not how they could make a living if compelled to move; so, fearing starvation, decided to send their fifteen-year-old leper son out into the cold world alone to beg his food, sleep in the open, and thus eke out an existence until death should claim him. They reasoned that he would soon die of his disease anyway, and it were better for them to stay in the village where they could live, than for the whole family to leave and all take the chance of starving to death.

Although this was fully explained to the son by his parents the little fellow could not get up courage enough to go out and face the dark future alone. In despair his parents decided to do away with him. They induced him to go down to the ocean with them, and taking the first opportunity, the father pushed the boy off from the top of a high rock into deep water. Thinking never to see him again, they returned to their home. The boy, however, accustomed to being in the water, managed to scramble out. With water dripping from his clothing he sneaked back home again; and then the astonished and disappointed mother decided to do her part. Securing the fearsome-looking general utility knife from the kitchen and brandishing it in the air, she threatened the life of her son if he did not leave home. Greatly frightened, he promised to leave next morning, but begged permission to stay over night. Next day he went forth he knew not where, but finally found his way to Taiku. At the time the Leper Hospital was filled to its capacity, as it always is, but we could not refuse him entrance. Three years' treatment with the chaulmoogra oil mixture in weekly doses of 9 c.c. hypodermically removed all his symptoms, and he was discharged as cured.

Last month the hospital evangelist preached in this boy's heathen village, and with the lad's co-operation won many converts. A new church was started consisting of eighteen men, mostly young, modernly educated, and very enthusiastic. Three years ago these villagers, thinking to protect their own lives, urged the parents to cast out their leper son. Little did they dream that the outcast would some day return, and still less could they have known he would come back with a cleansed body, no longer a menace to their lives, but a witness for Him Who came that they might have life and might have it more abundantly.

The adoption of the new treatment on a large scale soon began to have important consequences. What had hitherto been a work of mercy, giving food and shelter and the comfort of the Gospel to the suffering, now began to be a work of a different kind. It had largely been carried on by amateurs, in the best sense of that word, by people engaged in this demanding ministry out of the Christian love in their hearts. Now it would be no less compassionate in its attitude, but in its method it would gradually become more and more professional as the medical aspect of the work increased in importance and emphasis. This would inevitably bring about changes in policy, and some of these soon began to show themselves.

The first immediate result was the appointment of a Medical Secretary. This seemed to follow logically from the new approach. If the Mission was to become more and more involved in medical work, then clearly a medical man was required to advise the General Secretary and the Council on medical matters. The young doctor chosen bore a name already honoured in the Mission; his father, Dr. Thomas Cochrane, was a member of the Mission Council. The new Medical Secretary, Dr. Robert G. Cochrane, was to become even more widely known than his father as his contribution to the leprosy campaign gained world-wide recognition. But now he was just starting his long and distinguished career. He began in characteristic fashion by making a careful survey of the Mission's Homes in India, and submitting a report to the Council, the first of a long series of writings which have been of great value to workers in the leprosy field.

In this first report Dr. Cochrane graded the Mission's Homes in India. Class A institutions were those which should be developed to a high standard as leprosy hospitals and teaching centres. It was recommended that there should be six hospitals of this grade situated in strategic centres in India, and two in Burma—Mandalay and Moulmein. Purulia, the largest of the Mission's hospitals in India, was regarded as an example of a Grade A institution, and improvements were to be undertaken to make this hospital a pattern for others selected for up-grading. Grade B institutions were Homes which were not thought likely to rise to the standard of Grade A; they would continue to operate at their existing level with necessary replacements of buildings and equipment as time went on. Grade C Homes were much smaller, difficult to staff and uneconomic to maintain, and therefore might be closed at some convenient time in the future, suitable arrangements being made for the few remaining patients. Actually only one such Home was closed in the period ended 1934—that at Rurki.

This grading or classification of institutions was a helpful contribution to policy-making at the time (1926) and for many years beyond this date. Dr. Cochrane, however, did not wish to retain his appointment as Medical Secretary, and asked to be released from the staff of the Mission. Two years later he accepted a similar appointment under the auspices of what was then the British Empire Leprosy Relief Association (BELRA) but for a time he continued to give valuable help as Honorary Medical Adviser to the Mission.

It will be noticed that one of the functions of the Grade A institutions was that they should be developed as teaching centres. Patients and ex-patients were already being trained in a modest way to assist in the work, but now higher standards of efficiency would be required, and training courses would have to be instituted as part of the developing medical programme. Even more important, an advance in medical strategy would mean more doctors to lead the work. Where were they to come from? Medical missionaries were in short supply, and the co-operating Societies could not be expected to guarantee to provide qualified medical men in the numbers required. The solution to this problem must be found elsewhere. Accordingly the Secretary for India, Donald Miller, proposed that medical scholarships be made available to enable selected Indian Christian workers to gain medical qualifications. That was in 1929, and in the following year the Council agreed to provide three such scholarships, and authorized Mr. Miller to apply to the Miraj Medical School for the admission of three students sponsored by the Mission. The names of the three were Joseph Khan, P. Jacob Chandy, and N. Daniel. The Rev. Dr. Joseph Khan is still in charge at Subathu, a Justice of the Peace and the leader of the Christian community; Dr. Chandy's name is well known through his devoted service at Faizabad, Chandkhuri, Kathmandu, and Calicut. Although some scholarship holders have not fulfilled their early promise, the scheme has on the whole been markedly successful and has produced some outstanding leaders of the work in India, such as Dr. Victor P. Das, Secretary for Southern Asia, Dr. C. K. Job, and others whose names are not so well known to the general public.

The enthusiasm with which the new treatment was greeted was reflected in the attitude of the people most concerned, the patients themselves. In 1922 Dr. Thomas Cochrane reported to the Council following a recent visit to the Far East. Here is his testimony:

> The new treatment has changed the outlook. The people are clamorous for it. What yearning hope looks out from their eyes! The old despair has passed. The effect of the latest treatment on the morale of the Home is nothing less than a miracle. They are two hundred and thirty of the happiest, jolliest people you could come across—some of them with boundless energy.

The Home to which Dr. Cochrane was referring is not named. It may have been one of the China Homes, or possibly Fusan (now called Pusan) in Korea. A similar attitude on the part of patients was found in India. Dr. Isabel Kerr reported from Dichpalli at about the same time:

> The other day I noticed a patient who was slow in coming forward for his injection, and when asked the reason why, he said, 'I was saying grace before my medicine'. That is a fair indication of the spirit of all our work these days.

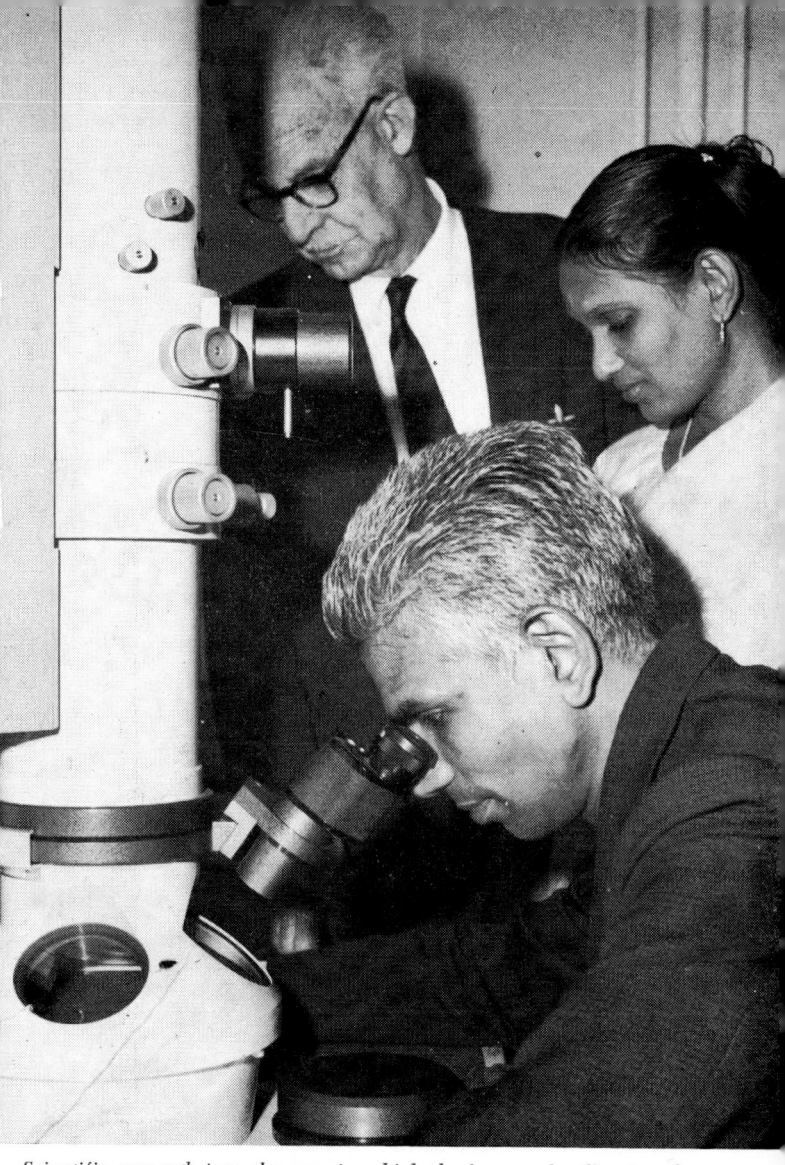

Scientific research into the way in which the leprosy bacillus invades the body and spreads is helped by such instruments as this powerful electron microscope, given to Vellore by The Leprosy Mission, and used by a member of the Mission's staff, Dr. C. K. Job, seen here with Mrs. Job and the late Dr. Neil Fraser, a pioneer of leprosy care.

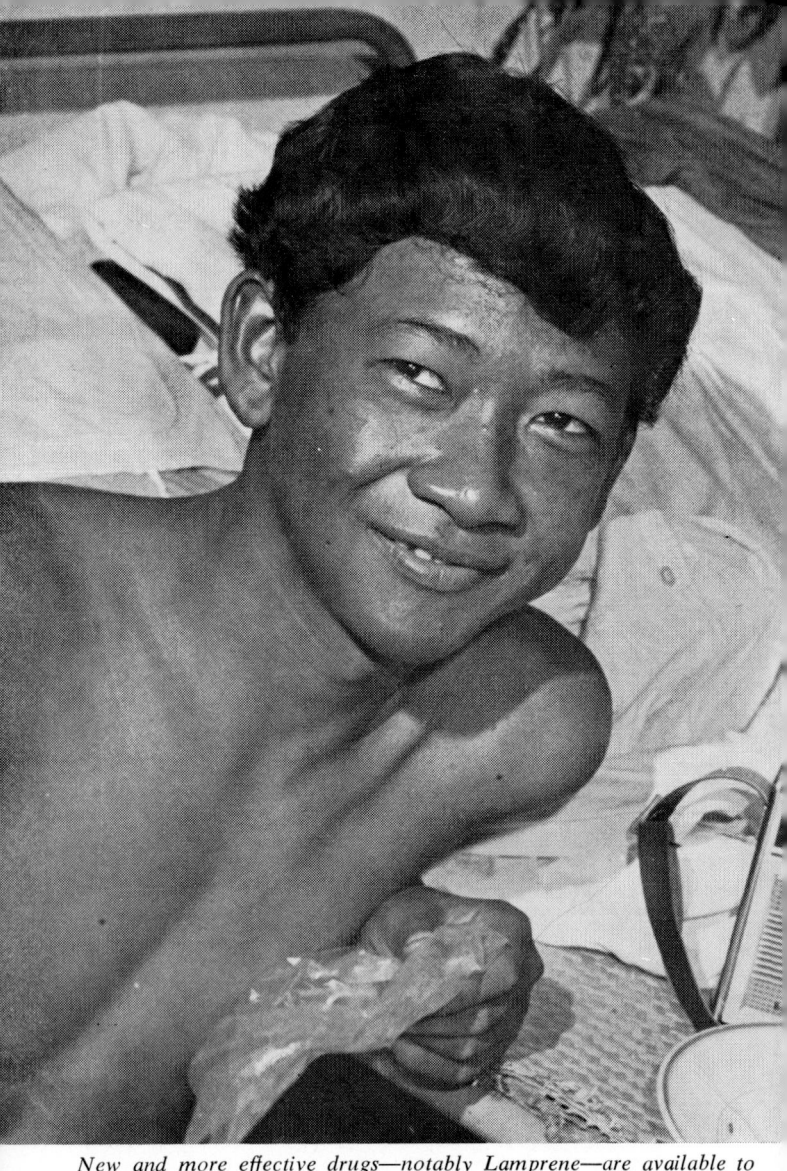

New and more effective drugs—notably Lamprene—are available to control cases where the patient is resistant to DDS. This young man, at Saiburi, Thailand, was desperately ill when first contacted, but Lamprene had worked wonders for him.

There is a new element in the psychology of the leper. The old apathetic hopelessness has passed, and in the case of our people here will never return unless, of course, treatment ceases. Only time will declare the full benefits this treatment brings, but there can be no question over the benefits now possible. If you can imagine a hospital, or home, full of patients who have good grounds for assurance that by medical skill they have been saved from certain death, then you may have some conception of the mental attitude of our people here. Naturally it is very exhilarating to live and work in such an atmosphere, and I enjoy my work better every day.

About seven years later the first glow of enthusiasm had faded to some extent, though a hopeful attitude still remained. The writer is Dr. V. Annaswamy, who through many years collaborated with Miss E. Lillelund in building up a fine work at Vadathorasalur:

We have given 7,105 injections to in-patients, and 2,940 to out-patients. Besides the hydnocreol we try also the sodium hydnocarpus solution both hypodermically and intravenously. We have seen marked improvements in those cases who were first treated with hydnocreol and then afterwards by the intravenous injections of 3 per cent solution of sodium hydnocarpus. We lay much stress on exercise. All the inmates take a very active part in cultivation. In spite of the scarcity of rain we were able to get something out of our gardens. Each ward has a beautiful flower garden much appreciated by visitors.

The writer then speaks of another aspect of life at Vadathorasalur:

Daily prayers are conducted in a temporary thatched shed of which a portion is used for storing firewood during the rainy season. Almost all the inmates attend the meetings regularly. A good spirit is prevailing among them. They can sing many lyrics by heart. Seventeen of the inmates, after a long period of probation as enquirers, and after a good confession of faith, were baptized on September 30th. They all took part in the service with a joyful heart. At present half of our inmates are Christians. We always pray to God to give us a church and increase the number of Christians. If anyone wants to see the happiest patients let them go to our asylum, especially at the Christmas season. Long before Christmas Day some of them will be busy cutting coloured papers for decoration, and some making their already tidy ward more tidy and white-washed; and in the evenings they will be singing Christmas carols with great enthusiasm.

Dr. Annaswamy went on to describe the celebration of the Christmas festival:

And now the Christmas season has gone, the gifts are getting old, but what remains imperished? It is the real joy, the joy that cannot be taken away by anybody, the joy which came purely by the Love of God through the birth of Christ, even to these neglected and outcast lepers, neglected by their own kith and kin. May this piece of work be a blessing to our land and progress to the glory of God!

In passing we note some points of interest: (*a*) the first mention of outpatients; (*b*) a reference to hydnocreol and sodium hydnocarpus, presumably two variants of the original hydnocarpus oil; (*c*) the emphasis on Christian teaching, to which we shall refer again in the next chapter. We note also the expression 'our asylum'. The Council had decided to drop the use of this word, but habit dies hard! Even so the general atmosphere described by the good doctor is very different from that which was once associated with the old word.

By the end of the period now under review oil therapy had had an extended trial, and in 1934 judgment was passed upon it:

It was not unnatural that after the complete pessimism of the past with regard to the treatment of leprosy, there should be a wave of exaggerated optimism when leprosy did come within the horizon of treatable diseases. One may sight a vessel on the horizon long before it comes to shore, especially if the winds are contrary. And we cannot yet say that treatment is so effective that the day has come when cure is possible for every leper. We cannot even say that every early case will be freed of the disease by treatment. We have repeated disappointments. Men and women and children are discharged with the disease arrested, and then later they return, the disease once more on the march. There is still very much to be done, both for those in whom the disease is still active and in the care of treated cases that no longer manifest any active symptoms. There is also a great deal to be done in developing preventative work.

Writing many years later, and with the benefit of hindsight, the Medical Consultant to the Mission, Dr. Stanley G. Browne, said:

The oil, hydnocarpus or chaulmoogra, was given by the mouth or by injection into the muscles or into the skin patches of leprosy. From the purified oil were prepared various compounds which were marketed by well-known drug houses, but the oil itself also continued to have a vogue. It did seem to do some good in leprosy, probably by encouraging repigmentation of pale skin patches and stimulating the body defences. In fact, research work is still being carried out on these and related effects of the oil. But in lepromatous leprosy it had very little, if any, action. We still awaited an active drug.

So it gradually became clear that 'the new treatment' was not after all the final and effective answer to the problem of leprosy. Even so the records of the period to the end of 1934 show clearly a general feeling of movement in what had been for so long a mainly static situation. There were new leaders coming forward, new methods being tried, and a new sense of direction. The result of this ferment of ideas would still lie in the future, but significant signs seemed to point to the possibility of real advance. In short, the sap was beginning to rise afresh in the Spreading Tree.

Chapter Five
JUBILEE

EARLY IN 1924 preparations began for the celebration of the Golden Jubilee of the Mission. To those supporters whose memories went back to the earliest days it must have seemed quite wonderful that the enterprise which had had so modest a beginning fifty years before should now have so much cause for thanksgiving and praise to God for prayers 'abundantly answered' and efforts 'crowned with success'. These are phrases taken from the magazine article describing the Jubilee meetings in London on September 30th, 1924, and they express the general tone of the meetings.

It was indeed 'one of the red-letter days in the history of the Mission'. After a morning Communion Service at St. Paul's, Portman Square, the Kingsway Hall was well-filled at afternoon and evening meetings under the chairmanship of the President of the Mission, the Most Rev. Dr. Charles F. D'Arcy, Lord Primate of Ireland. There were speakers representing India, Burma, China and the Home Base, and messages of greeting from The American Mission to Lepers, Inc., the newly formed French Committee of Help for Lepers, and a number of touching messages from patients.

But the message everyone wanted to hear was the word of Wellesley Bailey, who spoke at both meetings. Here is an extract from one of his addresses:

> I desire above all things that our meetings today should be meetings of praise. That is what we are here for, and I am glad and thankful that that note has been struck from the beginning. We are here to praise God for all the wonderful things that He has done for us during these fifty years. From the very first God seemed to set His seal upon the work, and that has been manifest in the blessing that has resulted on the efforts of His servants in ministering to the lepers. We thank God today for all the friends that He has raised up throughout the world for the Mission. We thank Him today for the splendid fellow-workers that we

have had from time to time, and those we have at the present moment. We thank Him for that great army of missionaries who, as a labour of love, have been, and are, ministering to the lepers in His Name. And I would like to say how much we appreciate also the hearty co-operation and fellowship of all the different Protestant Missionary Societies in this our work. This Mission to Lepers, I am accustomed to think, is 'a building not made with hands'. God has been the Builder thereof; and because of that fact, the Mission has gone on prospering, and will prosper. To His Name, His Name alone, we should give all the praise and glory today.

Ten years later the Diamond Jubilee was celebrated in a similar joyous manner on October 5th, 1934, in London with parallel meetings in Edinburgh and in Dublin. Once again distinguished speakers told of the work on the various fields and at the Home Bases. The London audience heard the Secretary for Australia, the Rev. F. A. Crawshaw, who had been specially invited to London to represent Australia and New Zealand at the Jubilee.

The founder of the Mission did not attend the London meeting this time 'owing to his advanced age', but he sent a characteristic telegram from his home in Edinburgh:

Founder's greetings; am with you in spirit today in rejoicing and thanksgiving.

There were again many messages of greeting and congratulation from institutions overseas. Here are one or two samples of the gratitude they expressed. First, part of the message from Purulia:

It is 60 years this 1934 since the springing up in your hearts came from God to found the Mission to Lepers. For 46 years by the great mercy of God we must personally testify the work here has gone regularly on. Turned out of their houses and villages and although beggars by the road and the shunned of all men and become the rejected of the world, because God put the desire into your minds we have all along been helped by good houses and a place of worship, good food and clothes and teaching and religious teaching arrangements and excellent medical arrangements and for this cause we now make manifest our hundred thousand thanks. Although we are utterly unworthy of receiving all these benefits because of the ever-present help of the infinite love of God please receive our unworthy thanksgivings. Please remember us in your prayers. We are able to give you nothing in return. Our humble prayer is that God will richly reward you. By the merits of your kindness please forgive all our mistakes in writing this. The end.

Purulia Leper Home Brethren.

The message from patients in China is worth quoting in full:

We have the honour to tell you that today we have heard that your honourable country's Leper Mission is remembering its sixtieth anniversary. The whole body of this Home is extremely happy and takes the opportunity to write a few characters to tell the honourable Mission that they may know that the Kutien Leper Home courteously acknowledges your abundant gifts for thirty-eight years. Very many of our brothers in this Home have by God's grace heard the doctrine of the Gospel and obtained the Lord's saving grace; therefore we write this letter to offer to your honourable Mission great, great, many thanks. Our whole body in this Home cannot repay your honourable Mission, but the whole body constantly prays hoping the Lord above, from the fulness of His grace, will great, greatly bless your honourable Mission, and all who help by their gifts. We also hope the Lord will open the way before you and greatly use this Leper Mission to lead very many sick people to the side of the Cross. We respectfully write this with one accord inviting the whole body of English London's Philanthropic and Charitable Leper Mission Society to glance at it.

The Middle Flowery People's Kingdom 23rd year, 4th month, 5th day.

The Middle Kingdom, Fukien, Kutien West Gate White Pagoda Relief Hall Leper Home whole body respectfully bends the neck.

Or again, from Soonchun in Korea.

> Borne down under the yoke of heavy agony and of sorrow and tears in an incurable disease, unable to overcome its eternal suffering, we, seven hundred patients, clothed upon with the warm loving zeal of you servants of God, having by the mercy of Jesus received treatment for our own worn bodies, and greater than that, having come to know the existence of God Whom we did not know, so that both body and soul which were about to die, have received the joy of a new life, how could we not be joyful? Having heard that this year is the Sixtieth Anniversary of the founding of your Mission to Lepers, we seven hundred who have received grace through the development of your work, weep tears of unspeakable joy and thanksgiving in congratulating you.

Some of the messages are quite long but there is no record of anything to equal a letter of thanks received by Mr. William Danner, General Secretary of the American Mission to Lepers, from Portuguese East Africa. It was fifteen feet long, written on the skin of a giant python!

In connection with these Jubilee celebrations two special publications were issued, the first in 1924, *Fifty Years' Work for Lepers* 1874-1924, and the second in 1934, *Sixty Years of Service on behalf of Lepers and their Children*. Taken together they provide an excellent survey of the work to date, and taken separately they reveal some interesting comparisons. It may therefore be well worth while to use them to examine some aspects of the Mission's life and work. The subject matter of both books is of high quality, most of it probably written by Mr. W. H. P. Anderson, the General Secretary. So we turn to him for many facts about the Mission's work in a period which otherwise might escape notice.

In retirement, Mr. Wellesley Bailey remained Honorary Superintendent of the Mission, and in 1924 the Honorary Treasurer was Sir William Fry, who was also Chairman of the Council. By 1934 the office of Treasurer was held by Colonel

G. C. Dobbs, O.B.E. 37 members of the Council are listed in the 1924 publication and 38 ten years later.

The 1924 book lists only three auxiliaries—Canada, Australia, and India, in that order.

In Canada the Secretary was the Rev. H. N. Konkle, who in 1922 succeeded Miss Lila Watt. Mr. H. J. Hannah continued to be the President and Honorary Treasurer of the Australian Auxiliary with the Rev. W. J. Eddy as Secretary. He retired in 1931.

The Rev. F. A. Crawshaw had already been invited to become Secretary for New Zealand, but actually took over the Australian constituency on the retirement of Mr. Eddy and is described as Secretary for Australia in the Diamond Jubilee book. In New Zealand there were two Honorary Secretaries in 1924—Mrs. Horne in the North Island, and Mr. Joseph Russell in the South Island. On the recommendation of Mr. Crawshaw a full-time Secretary for the whole of New Zealand was appointed in 1933—Mr. F. C. Perry, with headquarters in Auckland.

The American Committee is listed in detail in 1934 and is described as 'incorporated as the American Mission to Lepers', which was said to constitute 'the American branch of the Mission, and as such co-operates in the maintenance and development of the entire work of the Society', the President being Dr. William Jay Schieffelin and the Secretary Mr. William M. Danner. In the 1924 record there is a list of the members of the Indian Auxiliary Executive Committee headed by the Chairman, the Most Rev. Brooke Foss Westcott, D.D., Bishop of Calcutta and Metropolitan of India, and author of a prayer for the Mission which has been used widely for many years. Mr. A. Donald Miller is named as Honorary Secretary to the Indian Auxiliary. Ten years later the names of the members of the Committee are not given; the Chairman and the Honorary Secretary only are mentioned, and they remain the same as before.

Both in 1924 and in 1934 the Secretaries for England, Scotland, and Ireland are listed with other Secretaries at Headquarters, with no mention of Committee members. No doubt the reason was that all three Auxiliaries, as we should now call them, were represented directly on the Council. At a later stage, and in the case of England and Wales at a much later stage, all three attained full national Auxiliary status, each with its own Committee and its own constitution.

Switzerland is not mentioned in the two Jubilee lists, though a group of supporters in Zurich had been led for many years by Miss Margaret Grob until her death in 1924, and later by Miss Anna Grob and Miss Trumpler.

What did the financial support given by the Auxiliaries amount to? An answer is given in *Sixty Years of Service:*

> At the Jubilee of the Mission in 1924 the total amount received up to that time for the support of the work was £1,088,434. The amount received for the Mission's support in the sixth decade of its existence was £800,937, including net returns from the branches and auxiliaries overseas and grants and contributions received and expended on the field, making a total for the sixty years of £1,889,372. When we remember that the amount received in the first year was £579 12s. 10¾d., we realize how provision has been made for a constantly growing work and render thanks and praise to God for His unfailing mercies.

It is true that in recent years the total income of the Mission has increased so greatly that the two million pound mark has been reached in four years, or at most in five, compared with the 60 years referred to above. But such a comparison would be most unfair; conditions changed so much in the intervening years. It would be more just to say that the Mission had good reason for rejoicing. The total amount raised by the generosity of its friends was a remarkable achievement, especially when we remember that in 1934 the purchasing power of the pound sterling was so much greater than it is today.

Another factor contributing to the growing strength of the Spreading Tree was the service rendered by the missionary personnel of co-operating Societies. This was not merely an important contribution to the work, it was an essential one; the Mission had only one 'missionary' on the field—Donald Miller—and the training of national leaders was still in its early stages. On the other hand it may be said that many missionaries of the co-operating Societies offered their service very willingly. Leprosy work made a great appeal to them and they responded whole-heartedly, some of them giving many years of service to it.

Miss Rosalie Harvey's work is a notable example of this kind of devoted ministry. When she died in 1932 she had served the missionary cause in India for nearly fifty years, and 'founded and continued to serve until her death the Nasik Leper Home'. The Zenana Bible and Medical Mission, which she served, was one of thirty-five Missionary Societies co-operating with the Mission to Lepers in 1934.

The first example of co-operation with a Church Association or Society came at the end of the same year, and apparently too late for inclusion in the list detailed in the Diamond Jubilee publication. At the December meeting of the Council a proposal regarding the Manamadura Home made history. In response the Council agreed that the oversight of the Home, which the American Madura Mission had hitherto organized and controlled, should now pass to an Indian body, the Madura Mission Sangam, representing the Indian Church and the Christian community. It was an interesting development which seemed to hold great promise for the future.

In 1924 the list of institutions owned, managed, or aided by the Mission totalled 73, with 21 Homes in addition where provision was made for Christian teaching. By 1934 the corresponding figures were 89 Homes, with provision for Christian teaching at 21 Homes as before. Several new names appeared during the decade, among them Belgaum, Vadathorasalur, Cuttack, Dhamtari, and Saldoha in India, and Foochow, Tsinan-fu, and Chengtu in China. But the main reason for the increase between 1924 and 1934 was that Dr. Thomas Cochrane had presented a report on the incidence of leprosy throughout the world and had recommended that grants be made to a number of medical missionaries working in Africa.

In 1926 there appeared an article in the Mission magazine entitled 'Leprosy in Africa' stressing the need of this new field. The article went on to say that the Council had had this need under consideration for some time but felt that if it was to enter the African field it would require largely increased support. This was evidently forthcoming for by 1934 no fewer than 16 institutions in Africa were listed as receiving grants-in-aid from the Mission.

An early glimpse into one of these African stations is afforded by Dr. Stauffacher of Inhambane, Portuguese East Africa;

> Wasanea, a leper who was discharged from the Camp nearly six years ago, came in the other day and said, 'I don't suppose you know me.' I replied, 'Yes, I do'. But I must admit she was changed. She was nicely dressed and had two attractive baby girls of her own with her. 'I had to call and thank you again for what you have done for me,' she continued. 'Where would I be now if it were not for you? Somewhere in the jungles just suffering. And what would I look like now? I shudder to think of it.' 'So do I,' I replied. As I look at her happy face and healthy body I did not need to ask, 'Was it worth while?'. The girl then turned to blind Tom, who is without toes and without hands, and said, 'Are you happy?' 'Happy!' he replied. 'Where could I find a better place?' And his deformed face fairly shone as he said, 'And I love the Lord Jesus mightily.' He has been with us only five months, but he has found the secret of a happy life. We are not able to check the ravages of the disease in every case, but we can offer to all the knowledge, the riches, and the love of our Saviour.

And on the same page of the Mission magazine there is an appeal for £1,400 'for the lepers of Garkida, Nigeria . . . to make out-patient treatment available in a district where nothing has been done along the lines of leprosy relief'.

This extension of the Mission's work in Africa also partly accounts for a corresponding increase in the number of patients for whom the Mission had accepted responsibility. In 1924 the figures were: 'leper inmates' 7,850, healthy children 683; by 1934 these figures had risen to 14,800 and 900 respectively. The Spreading Tree was reaching out. But not, however, reaching out very far as yet. The emphasis was still on institutional work as being the most effective contribution which the Mission could make to the campaign against leprosy, leaving work in clinics and research largely to other agencies. But attention to outpatient work was being given in some places, and there is an indication of the shape of things to come in a reference in 1934 to 'the remarkably fine work being carried on in and around Swatow' in a series of up-country dispensaries organized by a medical missionary of the English Presbyterian Mission. His name was Dr. Neil Duncan Fraser, a name which will reappear later on in the Mission's story.

In the book about the Diamond Jubilee of 1934 work among children is dealt with separately for the first time. During the previous decade ten new Homes for children had been erected, three of them replacing buildings which had become too small, the other seven in response to the growing need. Some interesting stories about children are included in this section of the book, and there is a photograph of the first Leper Girl Guides Company at Cuttack.

From Cuttack comes the story of Samvari, who is described as 'a leper girl', though actually she was 26 years old at the time of this incident.

She had been a leper since she was three years old, and a life of misery and almost endless pain had left her devoid of hands and feet and soured in spirit. When I first knew her, says Mrs. Guest, I couldn't even get her to smile. Her face was a tragedy to look upon. Soon after we started the Guide Company, Samvari was watching a Guide, a Mohammedan girl, struggling through her knots for the Tenderfoot test. 'That's not the way to do the fisherman's knot,' said Samvari. 'Well, I'm sure *you* couldn't do it!' said the indignant Guide. 'I may have no hands, but I can, and *will* do it,' was the reply; and out Samvari went and got an iron hook which was fastened to the end of the well rope. She insisted upon the Guide bandaging the hook on to the stump of her right arm, and with a stick of firewood strapped to the other stump and a piece of rope, Samvari struggled on until she had done the fisherman's knot. On the strength of that achievement she joined the Guide Company and became one of the finest Guides I have ever met. She was later awarded the Nurse Cavell Badge by the Girl Guide Headquarters. This is looked upon as being the Girl Guides' 'Victoria Cross', and is only given to Guides who bear pain with extreme fortitude and pluck. On the last Sunday I had with the lepers at Cuttack, we took Communion together, and Samvari with several other Christian Guides was there. It was our custom, as each received the little portion of bread from the hands of the padre, to repeat a verse of Scripture, and Samvari, her white sari spread over her two stumps of hands, said, 'I bear in my body the marks of the Lord Jesus'. And truly she did so. I shall never take Communion again without remembering her.

After that date of 1928 Guide Companies were formed at several Homes both among the healthy and infected girls. At Purulia it was among the girls with leprosy that the 1st Purulia Girl Guide Company was formed. Miss Thornton tells how this came to be.

In January 1928 the girls heard of the great Sisterhood of the Guides. They were told their work and play of the previous year had been leading up to the formation of a Company among them. They were given a week to think over what it meant to become a Guide and invited to come forward the following Monday to begin their training in real earnest. Such a happy crowd with smiling clean faces greeted one the following week, every girl in the Home eager to join the great Sisterhood. They were divided into three patrols—Rose, Phlox, and Marigold. Later the girls in the Observation Ward were invited to join, eight coming in—the Sunflowers. The Company was registered in May, 1928, and a little later in the year Phulmoni, prachina (head) of House No. 5, had received her warrant as Lieutenant . . . Most of the girls can take all the tests necessary for tenderfoot and 2nd class, with the exception of running or skipping. The Marigold Patrol are chiefly the crippled girls, but so far they have managed to do the same things as the other girls. It takes them much longer to tie knots or sort out pieces of the Union Jack, for instance; but it gives them immense joy to think they can do what the others are doing.

Miss Thornton goes on to speak of the formation of the 2nd Purulia Company, when some of the healthy girls asked if they could not also become Guides. So the work was established at this particular station, and it flourished for many years, and still goes on. There had been a couple of Scout Troops before this, but with the starting of Guides a new impetus was given to the movement and by 1934 there were Scout Troops in many Homes.

Before passing on to another subject we may well pause to reflect that the fact that Guide training was begun and continued at Purulia through the years was an important factor in a situation which Miss Thornton could never have imagined. Some fourteen years after the establishment of the Guide Companies it was a compass used in their training at Purulia that guided a boat over a wide and lonely sea, and so played a decisive part in the dramatic story subsequently told in Donald Miller's remarkable book *A Ship! A Ship!*

Last of all, but by no means least, there is the remarkable continuing story of the spiritual fruits of the ministry of so many devoted workers. In 1924 there were said to be 7,850 patients and 683 healthy children in the Homes, as has already been noted; the new fact to be added is that no less than 6,027 of them, adults and children taken together, were said to be Christians. This is a very high percentage, and during the following decade there was no falling off, for by 1934 it is stated that 'there are upwards of 10,500 Christian lepers' in the Mission's own and aided Homes 'and in those institutions where it provides for Christian services and teaching.' Certainly this teaching was in many cases very thorough.

In the 1933 magazine there was an article on the Church life of the Bethesda Home, Champa, written by the Rev. P. A. Penner. First there was a description of the Sunday morning service in the Bethesda Church. Sunday School took place in the afternoon with ten classes for patients of all ages. There was a Bible Class on Tuesday afternoons and a weekly prayer meeting on Fridays. Candidates for baptism were given a course of instruction before being admitted to Church membership. There was also a quarterly meeting at which all the business of the Church was discussed, and every day in the afternoon there were visits to the very sick. This programme of Christian work had many parallels in India and in other countries. And it produced wonderful results—not only the preaching and teaching but the day-to-day effect of a ministry most lovingly carried on in the spirit of Christ. Whatever the determining factor, a rich harvest was reaped, and the hearts of many Christian workers, national as well as missionary, were made glad.

Even non-Christian patients who did not finally accept Christ were nevertheless responsive to the Christian spirit so evidently at work around them. This was clear when from time to time they joined in with Christian patients in answer to a call for help from some area stricken by flood or famine, and in at least one case in response to an appeal for a Christian agency. Donald Miller, at that time Secretary for India, had been visiting Naini in the course of one of his tours, and had this story to tell in his report to London.

At Naini, just before my visit, they had had their annual offering for the British and Foreign Bible Society. It was announced one Sunday that during the week Mr. Mackenzie (the Manager) would receive their offerings, and the following Sunday at the morning gathering in the church the total was announced. Mr. Mackenzie got up and said that he had much pleasure in announcing that a sum of Rs. 212 (about £15 sterling) had been contributed. 'But however did they raise such a sum?' exclaimed Mrs. Higginbottom, the missionary, knowing that it did not even include her own and Dr. Higginbottom's contributions. 'They had a meeting and decided that they would give up the whole of one week's cash allowance for their purchase of supplies,' said Mr. Mackenzie. 'But what about the non-Christians?' asked Mrs. Higginbottom. 'It wouldn't be right for the meeting to decide for everybody, when we have Hindus and Mohammedans among our guests. Are you sure that they too wanted to help this Society for spreading the news of the Bible?' Then up stumbled a Mohammedan inmate at the back of the church. 'Memsahib,' he said, 'we, too, have joined in gladly. We are not Christians, but we know that it is because of the teaching of your Bible that you are caring for us, and that friends in many lands are saving us from starvation. But for the Bible and its message what would be our fate? Because of the Bible what good fortune is ours! It is a good book, and we are glad to help a little the Society which is making the Bible known throughout the world.'

Of the patients who became Christians, some found it hard to live up to the Christian ideal, and some fell away. There were also the great saints among these humble, suffering people, members of 'The Fellowship of the Tenth Leper', as Donald Miller called it, and about whom he wrote in his book *Music at Midnight*. And from time to time there occurred what might well be called miracles of grace.

Mr. W. C. Irvine, of Belgaum, had to deal with an idea deeply embedded in the Hindu mind, and therefore difficult to eradicate. This is the concept of caste, that stratification of Hindu society in classes so rigidly bounded that none may pass from one stratum to another. Moreover it was not merely a matter of the boundaries existing between one caste and another caste, or between high caste and low caste; it also directly concerned the even greater division between caste and 'untouchable' or outcaste.

Three Marathas and a Mahar—the former caste people, and the latter a low caste—were sent to us from Satara by the Local Board in 1913. Two of these are with us today, two have died. One, a woman, never gave us assurance of becoming a Christian; she died two or three years after coming. The Mahar, blind Balu, who passed away in 1921, was, I believe, the first inmate to become a

Christian in this Asylum, and went on well to the end. Hari, one of the Marathas, though still with us, is very near his end. He was baptized, after a dream or vision of the Saviour, some years ago, and is now looking for his call—longing for it. The disease has a sorry grip of his poor body, and we hope that he will soon get his release.

When Hari was about to be baptized, Ragoba, with some others, declared that if only we would have a separate meeting for caste men, a separate breaking of bread, they would *all* be baptized. We showed him the impossibility of this, and he showed us the impossibility of *their* eating with low caste Christians—at that time Balu and two other former low caste men had been baptized. Years passed; Hari and other caste men were baptized and brought into fellowship; but Ragoba, though often declaring that he believed in Christ, would go no further. Some months ago, at the close of a meeting, he said he wished to be baptized. I conversed with him on two or three occasions afterwards, and he seemed clear enough—but some of the Christians told me that he never would be really one of them. It appeared that he intended to be baptized, but not to partake of the Lord's Supper. One or two Sundays ago a fellow missionary, after preaching the Gospel, asked whether any would accept Christ as their Saviour. He had been speaking of the danger of delay, and on the invitation being given Ragoba spoke up boldly, saying that he accepted Christ and wanted to be baptized. This time he was in real earnest, and with two others he was 'buried with Christ' last Thursday. Afterwards the once proud caste man was found seated humbly with eleven others at the table of the Lord. Among the twelve were two of the original three low caste Christians, with whom it was *quite impossible* for a caste man to feast together! But 'My grace *is* sufficient'.

A fitting word with which to close this first part of the story of the Spreading Tree.

Part Two

THE TREE WITHSTANDS THE STORMS
(1935 - 1945)

Chapter Six
THE LULL BEFORE THE STORM

THE YEARS FROM 1935 to 1940 can now be seen as a deceptively quiet lull before the storm broke with the onset of the Second World War.

As the clouds gathered in a darkening sky there was growing concern in the West. But in the Far East there was war already. William Anderson made one of his long tours in 1935 and 1936, visiting India, the Straits Settlements, China, Japan and Hong Kong (where he called on the Director of Medical Services to discuss treatment of leprosy, including provision for advanced cases on a smaller island to be set apart for the purpose—an interesting hint of things to come some 15 years later).

The report gives no hint of trouble in the Far East. In China he visited several stations, including the new leprosarium recently built by the Chinese Mission to Lepers, and the Home at Hangchow; he and Dr. Maxwell discussed schemes for development of the Mission's work in China. Few, if any, of these schemes came to fruition. As for Japan, two-and-a-half days were spent in Tokyo in talks with Dr. Oltmans, Secretary for Japan of the American Mission to Lepers. Very little detail is given in this part of the tour report, and no indication of special difficulties. Yet in the very next year (1937) the new leprosarium at Shanghai is reported as being evacuated to temporary premises elsewhere 'owing to heavy fighting in the area', though the Council Minute does not say who the combatants were. This is made clear in a report written by Dr. Stephen D. Turten:

> This is being written in April, 1941, four years all but three months since the commencement of the Sino-Japanese hostilities, and during these four years Hangchow has been almost continuously within sound of the guns. The city was occupied by the Japanese on Christmas Eve, 1937, the front remained within three miles of the city until January, 1940, and since that date has been about six miles distant. On a hill just outside the city, alongside the C.M.S. Branch

Hospital for Tuberculosis, stands the Leper Hospital which was founded in 1887 by the late Dr. D. Duncan Main. It consists of two main Hospital Buildings, one for men and one for women, with their little church, St. John's Chapel, between them almost on the edge of a cliff. Lower down in the compound are two small bungalows for men patients. There are at present 98 patients in Hospital, but this does not mean that they are 'hospital patients' in the ordinary sense of bedridden people. It is true that over sixty per cent are suffering from some kind of deformity because they have come too late to get the full benefits which accrue from modern treatment, but the majority are able to get about the place and lead a more or less happy life.

The slogan in England, 'Dig for Victory', has found its counterpart here in the lepers' compound. Formerly we used to allow the patients a definite sum of money each month with which to cater for themselves, but the war upset this plan and all suffered from price fluctuations, while some suffered from unwise use of money. Our solution was that the Hospital should provide a suitable menu for all as far as conditions permit. Rice which used to cost $8 or $9 for a Chinese hundredweight now costs $128, and flour which used to cost $3 a bag now costs $28. Under these conditions we have found that the only way is for the Hospital to supply a definite ration of food by weight rather than by price, and for the patients not to handle the money. At the same time the patients who are sufficiently able-bodied to work are co-operating with us by cultivating almost every inch of the grounds. We allow them the use of the land free and buy their vegetables at half-market rate. This means cheaper buying for the Hospital, enough work to keep the patients happy and out of mischief, and pocket money for them to use.

So it was war between Japan and China at that time, and Dr. Sturton's picture of Hangchow in wartime vividly suggests what life was like in this beleaguered place. At the time Mr. Anderson visited the station the situation was not so critical as it later became, but it seems strange that he makes no mention of Japanese aggression leading to the attack on China, the setting up of the puppet state of Manchukuo, and the withdrawal of Japan from the League of Nations. As for Korea, in 1940 there was an emergency meeting of the Council in August (just before the Battle of Britain) to discuss the intended closing of the Home at Fusan (Pusan) which was said to be required by the Japanese authorities 'for military purposes'.

In the meantime there was a real lull in India and Burma, the Mission's main field of work and chief centre of interest. A number of minor projects were taken up, such as houses at Dhamtari and Kothara, extension of the hospital dispensary at Naini, improvements to the water supply at Purulia, a house for the resident manager at Tenghsien, and so on. Vadathorasalur rejoiced in the new church for which Dr. Annaswamy and the patients had prayed, and a lovely building it was. Extensions were considered at the Naini Home, including the provision of a new medical block. In 1938 Purulia celebrated its Golden Jubilee, and at Chandkhuri the Nottrott gateway was erected as a memorial to its founder.

The 1940 magazine carried an article on the Happy Mount Colony in Formosa established by Dr. G. Gushue-Taylor. There was a peaceful atmosphere in the Colony in spite of the nearness of both China and Japan.

About this time there was a grant to Valbonne which is noteworthy because this institution in France is described as 'a sanatorium for lepers', the first time the word 'sanatorium' is used in the Minutes of the Council. Valbonne is referred to in the Diamond Jubilee book as an example of international co-operation.

> It was through a special gift made by the American Mission to Lepers that the beautiful mediaeval monastery, La Chartreuse de Valbonne, was purchased and reconditioned as a home for the lepers of France, under the supervision of the French Mission to Lepers.

In short, the general atmosphere was one of quiet, steady progress.

Many stories of these years confirm this impression. At Fusan (Pusan) in Korea, for instance, Christmas was celebrated in the traditional style, and Mrs. Mackenzie gives a lively account of the Christmas-tree party in the Healthy Children's Home:

The big event of Christmas Day to them is to gather at the missionary's home for a Christmas-tree party. Perhaps that part of Christmas is the happiest to the missionary and his family too, for from the time they arrive with the Home foster-father and mother, the beaming faces of the children radiate an infectious happiness. Shoes are slipped off—Korean fashion—at the door (and what fun Carlo, the pup, had playing with a few that had unwisely been left outside!) and in they trip and take their places at the table. Sharp, excited eyes glance from the Christmas tree in the corner to the good things on the table, but no-one attempts to touch food until their Heavenly Father has been thanked. Fervent 'Amens' from one and all unite with the one who has offered their thanksgiving and then the fun begins! You should see how quickly their cups empty! Sometimes we think they must enjoy the tea (it is the only time during the year that they get it) more than the eatables, they pass up their cups for so many refills. Sipping it with a spoon is quite correct Korean manners and hot tea can be disposed of much quicker that way, can it not?

The Good Samaritan story told by Donald Miller in *An Inn called Welcome* has been repeated many times in the history of the Mission. On one such occasion it was the Scouts at Raniganj who came to the rescue.

Jogesh Chowdhuri, aged about forty, found that his leprosy was getting so bad that he could hardly walk as a result of his bodily weakness and the ulcers that were on his feet. He lived in a little out-of-the-way village and had never heard of a home where lepers could be cured. But he had heard that the god in another village was very powerful, and could cure leprosy if he was propitiated in the right way. So Jogesh determined to make the pilgrimage to this god, and set out on the long and painful journey with a young boy as his companion. When he reached the village where the god was, he made many offerings and repeated many prayers, but though he remained there for some time he got no better. At that time he heard of the Raniganj Leper Home, and as the god could do him no good he determined to go there. But it was a terrible journey. He had to beg his way, and live on the little food that people gave him, and could hardly crawl along, so weak had he become and so sore were his feet. After many days he reached Raniganj and there collapsed under a big banyan tree. He still received small quantities of rice from passers-by, and thus managed to keep alive, but he could not move forward another inch. And the Home and the doctor were about two miles away.

After he had been there for about four days, one of the Mission workers passed by, and Jogesh managed to attract his attention and told him his story. Of course he would be taken into the Home, but how was he to get there? No-one would touch the leper, and he was truly a repulsive sight, with his filthy rags and thin, diseased body with all the bones showing. What could be done? Then he remembered—the Scouts! Hastily scribbling a note to the Home—'S.O.S. Scouts wanted'—he went on his way, confident that on his return that way Jogesh would no longer be begging under the tree. And he was not. The Scouts got the note, and carrying a 'charpoy' (a light string bed), they went to the tree by the river where Jogesh was and soon carried him to the Home. There his troubles were ended, for he was put into the hospital ward and soon began to mend with proper care. He is still very thin and weak, but he can walk about now and is cheery. He says he wants to leave the hospital ward and go into one of the other houses.

And even in the valley of the shadow a triumphant faith shines forth. Dr. W. F. Joseph, of Chevayur, Calicut, tells the story of 'a Servant of Jesus', which is the meaning of the man's name.

Jesudasan, the 18-years-old new convert, was suffering patiently on his death-bed. How calmly and with what amount of hope he looked forward to the departure of his soul for the enjoyment of Heavenly pleasures only a few can realize. Even while he was living and the pangs of his dire disease had tightly and cruelly held him, he began to realize the sweetness of the love of Jesus as his Redeemer and Saviour. He could well experience and even tell his friends and associates of the lightness of his heart and his personal experience of the forgiveness of sins. He knew his hour of death was at hand, and so did his friends; one of them asked him curiously where his soul was destined to go. On hearing this question he smiled and before he could answer incoherently, they could well guess what they would hear. With a heart filled with joy he said, 'Don't you know . . . where . . . I shall go? . . . I go to my Lord and Saviour. Oh! I see Him . . . calling me.'

By contrast with what was soon to follow as the storm of war burst in its fury, here is a picture of the varied activities carried on at Moulmein in Burma.

To everyone who can work something is given, as often as possible. To able-bodied men there is the heavier work. The cleaning of the compound, the cleaning of their own rooms, the cooking of their own food, and other tasks that are not too heavy are given to practically all the folks except the blind and badly crippled. One man does the carpentry that is needed about the Home and is now asking for more tools that he may train some of the younger men and boys in the carpentry skills. Another man supervised and many helped in the laying of lime concrete for the cookhouse floors. Some have regular duties as ward servants, for which they are paid a small sum extra. All the oiling of the buildings was done with leper labour, and done cheaply and well. A new fence needed to keep cattle out of the compound was erected by them. A large area covered with bushes was cleared. Even the badly crippled ones can swat an incautious fly, and have been given the task of keeping down the pests. The women are overjoyed with a loom, and the carpenter has made a second one which will soon be in use. Gardens have been attempted in a small way, but more can be done. Plenty of fresh vegetables are greatly to be desired, and this side of our Home life can be greatly improved. Goats are kept by individuals, but we hope to make this a community affair in the near future when proper fencing can be put up. Cows have been promised us and we await with eagerness this new activity, which is so much needed for adding milk to the diet of the sick.

All too soon this busy, happy place was to be engulfed in the tide of invasion, and the Medical Officer at Moulmein, Dr. Nitiyand Dass, reported to be 'in enemy hands'.

During a period of increasing tension it was not to be expected that there would be many fresh advances. Only two such projects are referred to in the Minutes of the Council in the years 1935 to 1940. Dr. David Hynd, a medical missionary of the Church of the Nazarene, Swaziland, made proposals for the establishment of a new Leprosy Home at Mbuluzi, Swaziland. The Council approved the scheme in 1938 and made an initial grant for buildings together with a small recurring annual grant. The other piece of new work was a very much larger project involving capital expenditure of several thousand pounds and considerable maintenance costs in succeeding years.

The scheme in question was the plan to build a complete new Home and Hospital at Faizabad in the United Provinces (now Uttar Pradesh), North India. At an early date the Council had been considering the extension of the Naini Home, as we have already mentioned, but circumstances arose drawing attention to the possibility of new work at Faizabad, about a hundred miles from Naini but serving the same area of need and relieving pressure on the older institution. There were one or two interesting features of the new scheme.

One was certainly the origin of the project. Faizabad was the first example of a new call to action coming to the Mission from outside Church and Mission circles. The first move was not made by a Christian, but by a high-caste Hindu official, a gentleman of liberal outlook and broad sympathies who was concerned about the leper beggars who congregated at Ajodhya, a centre of Hindu pilgrimage within the Faizabad municipal boundary, and desired to get these people off the streets of the town. Hence came the suggestion that the Mission should join the local authorities in solving the problem. The first reply was that the Mission was not interested in a scheme for mere segregation as such. A much more thorough-going project would be required to enlist the help of the Mission, involving the establishment of a modern leprosy hospital and treatment of the disease, rather than merely shutting away those who suffered from it.

On his way home from China W. H. Anderson called at

Faizabad and talked to the authorities, with the result that shortly after his visit the Commissioner at Faizabad formally invited the Mission to undertake this modern scheme, offering financial assistance as well as a site. There were also negotiations with the Medical Department of the Government of the United Provinces which ended with the assurance that the Government would support the scheme by making the usual capitation grant (*i.e.,* an agreed monthly sum for patients in residence).

The co-operation of the local missionary organization (the Methodist Missionary Society) was also secured in respect of the management of the proposed Home and its pastoral oversight through the local Methodist Church. But there was at that time no missionary of this Society available and competent to undertake the considerable task of erecting the first block of buildings. So in the end the Secretary for India, Donald Miller, agreed to leave his office at Purulia and live at Faizabad near to the chosen site, where he and his wife spent about a year.

> Up till now, in the case of the older Homes, the work was confined to a few simple buildings at the start, and later additions were made as the needs of the work required and as further funds became available. It would obviously be unfair to say that there was little or no planning in the earlier years, for as each additional building was constructed its relation to existing buildings was naturally considered. So there grew up a kind of plan adjusted from time to time as the needs of the Home increased. Older institutions of this type which are the property of the Mission have been extensively enlarged and improved in recent years, and in some cases have been almost entirely rebuilt in accordance with the modern idea of what a leprosy hospital ought to be. Yet even so the new modernised plan is a modification and extension of the old. Faizabad was the first Leprosy Home owned by the Mission which was built to a plan conceived before a single brick was laid on the site.

On August 17th, 1938, the new Hospital and Home was formally opened by the Governor of the United Provinces,

Sir Maurice Hallett. In 1944 he went again to the Home, accompanied by Lady Hallett, and wrote in the Visitors' Book some encouraging remarks on what he saw. Praise from Sir Maurice was praise indeed, for he was not accustomed to handing out flattering bouquets. Many other visitors at various times have been equally impressed and all have realized the fine work done by Dr. P. J. Chandy in the early years of this new Home. He had given life to an admirable plan and had effectively used the resources at his disposal to create what was at that time a model institution for the treatment of sufferers from leprosy.

The Faizabad scheme has been described in some detail because it set a kind of pattern for other schemes which were to follow. Just as the medical work tended to become more professional, so also planning had to rise to a higher standard. The rather haphazard ways of earlier years now began to give way to a more considered policy, and this Faizabad scheme indicates most of the main lines of future planning.

First of all there must be a careful survey of the need in a particular area and an equally careful assessment of the resources required to meet that need. Then there must be consultation with the Government of the country concerned to win Government goodwill and if possible Government financial support. Next the co-operation of the local church, or mission, if any, must be secured.

Another piece of planning of a different kind, on a smaller scale and involving comparatively little expenditure, was the building of Santiniketan (the word means 'The Abode of Peace') at Purulia. It was to be a small house in which groups of girls would actually live in turn and thus learn useful lessons in housekeeping and community living. But first the house had to be built. Donald Miller had already received some money, but who was to plan and who was to build? The answer was—the children themselves.

> So we all got together. What was the plan to be? What was it going to cost? We divided the bigger boys and girls (about 40 in all) into four little companies. Each was to draw its own plan of what it thought would be a model

house, and then make a model to scale. The models were really extraordinarily good. Then came a council to consider them. Doors, windows, position of rooms, all were scrutinized. We tried to incorporate the best of each. One had a tiny little prayer room; yes, we must try to get that in. Another had a better planned stores than the others. We must use that. And so from the four models we arrived at a fifth plan, and a model to scale was made of that. Then we began counting the cost. Ideas were terribly vague. So inquiries had to be made. What did tiles cost per thousand? How many would be needed to cover such and such an area? And what about the wood? A master must take some of the boys away into the country where they could buy cheaper than in the town—a glorious all-night adventure travelling along in a slow bullock cart! At last estimates were worked out by the four companies. They varied from about Rs. 150 to Rs. 180 (about £10 or £12 at the current rate of exchange).

Then began the actual building, and the children had a wonderful time, bringing water, kneading the mud with their feet, building the walls. Mr. Miller says that any day before or after school, which of course had to go on as usual, you could hear a happy band of boys and girls shouting away as they built like children at the seaside building castles!

A boys' carpentry class, working under the head carpenter of the Leper Home, got busy with door and window frames. Soon we began to see the cottage really going up, and the mud walls climbing up to the level of the roof. In October, the month the roof went on, I was away. A little more outside help for a few days had to be introduced for the heavy rafter work and the tile laying ... If only they could have the roof on before my return! And so they did, and greeted me with beaming delighted faces.

Six days later the Governor of the Province was to visit the Home. Would the cottage be ready by then? Would he even open it for them? Such an important man to open such a little cottage?

Then the Governor came, straight from a big Darbar, with its glittering silver throne and wonderfully dressed attendants, red carpets, and everything splendid, to this humble little mud cottage, and declared it open. And he was delighted to do so.

But one thing more remained. The Governor had declared the cottage open, but there must be God's blessing invoked by the Minister before it was occupied. In a week's time the Rev. Mr. Sharpe was to return. So we waited for him, and two days after his arrival the *Protishta* or dedication ceremony took place. It was a happy gathering when we had our service with the boys and girls our hosts and hostesses. With song and prayer we invoked God's blessing. Now the house is occupied. Each week four fresh girls go in. They have a week's money given them, and do their own budgeting and buying and cooking and cleaning. There are lots of things still to learn, lots to do. But therein lies the joy of living.

Along with other activites of the Mission the medical work went on and gradually increased in importance. Although the experts were beginning to doubt the real effectiveness of oil therapy, chaulmoogra and hydnocarpus oil and their derivatives still held the field as the standard treatment; the Madras Government placed such faith in this treatment that it proposed to make grants only to 'treatable' cases, and not to the so-called 'burnt-out' cases. This might mean that possibly half the patients in the Mission's Homes in the Madras Presidency would be classified as non-treatable, and therefore no Government grant would be received for them. The Council in reply said that it 'could not accept any condition that would restrict the admission into its Homes of destitute and suffering lepers irrespective of whether they were likely or not to receive treatment of their disease'. This was a courageous answer which later cost the Mission dear as it had to accept the financial implications of this policy. But as the argument went on for years beyond the period now under study the matter must be left there for the present with the comment that in this case the compassionate attitude prevailed over the then scientific view, at least in the Council's thinking.

The policy of granting medical scholarships to selected Indian workers was continued, and several awards were made in the period 1936 to 1940. The most notable of these scholarship holders was a Mr. Victor P. Das who began his medical studies in 1937.

More could be said about the medical work at this period of time but we must be content with an extract from an address at the 1935 Autumn Conference in London. The speaker was Dr. Ernest Muir, and in view of the date of his remarks, this may truly be called a prophetic word.

> The home of leprosy is the village. A great many cases are found in the towns; but these are very largely people who have gone from the villages to work in the towns. Very often they were infected with leprosy before they went to the towns, and there under the hard economic conditions the disease developed. And again, there is another class who go to the large towns—the begging lepers who are found in almost all the large towns in India. But the real home of leprosy is the village. Now we might go on for years, for centuries, one might say, treating those who come to the leper homes or who come to the dispensaries for outpatient treatment, but the disease would never tend to diminish because the real source of the disease would still remain. In future the main stress must be laid on preventive work in the villages themselves; and especially on the prevention of child infection, for children are more susceptible to leprosy than adults, and it is those who acquire the disease in childhood who become the infectious cases in the next generation.

For a good many years it had been a source of strength that so eminent a leprologist should be so closely associated with the work of the Mission. This eminence was officially recognized for the third time in 1937. Dr. Muir already held the Kaiser-i-Hind gold medal and bar; now he was further honoured with the award of the C.I.E. Another honour richly deserved was the award of the Kaiser-i-Hind gold medal to the Secretary for India, Mr. A. Donald Miller. This gave great pleasure to the Mission as a whole, and not least to the Indian staff.

Even so, the highest place could well be given to an award of a lower degree, and this to a person of whom most friends of the Mission today may never have heard. This was the Kaiser-i-Hind silver medal awarded to Mr. Pitale of Naini in 1937. What was so special about Mr. Pitale? Simply this, that he was an ex-patient, the first or perhaps the only one to be honoured in this way. He had for many years acted first as a laboratory technician and then as head of the Naini laboratory staff. He had not only carried out thousands of laboratory tests himself, but had also trained no fewer than thirty-eight other technicians. By 1936 his health was failing and in July of that year he was obliged to give up this work.

On the wider front there was a meeting of the International Leprosy Congress in 1938. There had previously been three international conferences of this kind—the first in Berlin in 1897, the second at Bergen in 1907, and the third at Strasburg in 1923. This fourth Congress was held at Cairo under the auspices of the Egyptian Government. The Mission was represented by the General Secretary and the Secretary for India. The Rev. J. Noble Mackenzie, superintendent of the Pusan Home in Korea, broke his journey home for furlough and also attended the Congress on behalf of the Mission. There were upwards of three hundred delegates, representing 55 countries, and no doubt the reason for this large attendance, much larger than at previous conferences, was the increased interest in leprosy being taken by Governments in many parts of the world now that the disease was regarded as being capable of treatment. Leading figures at the Congress were Dr. Ernest Muir, Dr. John Lowe, and Dr. Robert Cochrane, and in his article about the Congress, Donald Miller drew attention to the fact that all three of these distinguished leprologists had a missionary background. This tradition has been maintained in the years that followed as to this list of missionaries or ex-missionaries there were added the names of Dr. Paul Brand, Dr. Stanley Browne, Dr. Frank Davey,

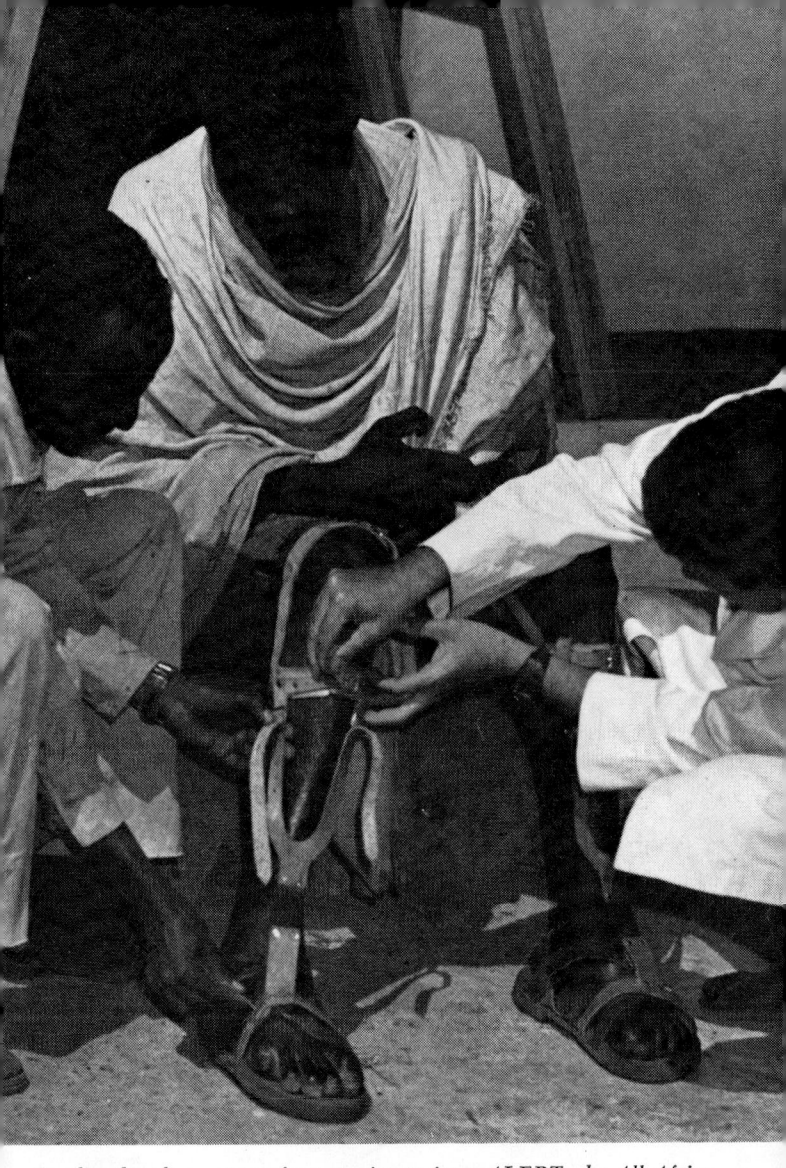

Lending hands to save a foot—a picture from ALERT, the All-Africa Leprosy and Rehabilitation Training Centre at Addis Ababa, Ethiopia.

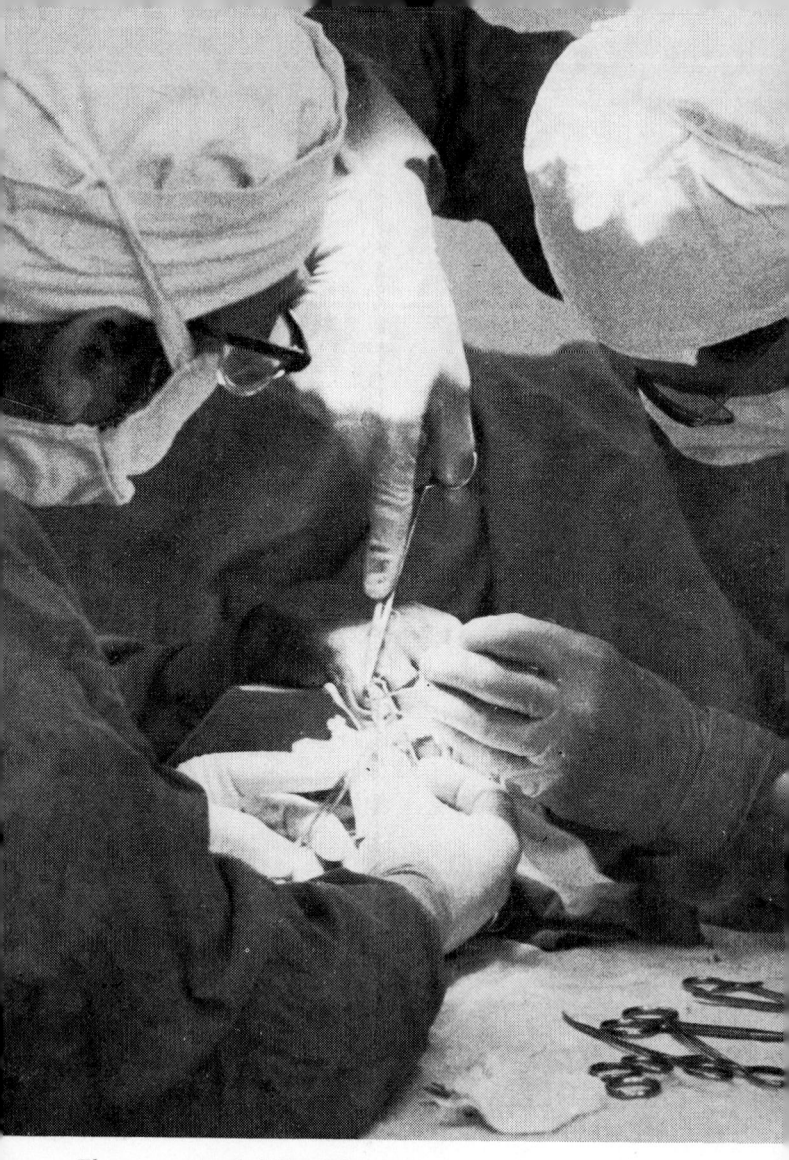

The concentrated skills of the surgeon and his team restore movement to immobilized fingers—a photo from ALERT, in Addis Ababa.

Dr. Neil Fraser and Dr. Oliver Hasselblad, to mention some who come immediately to mind. The missionary motive has been a crucial factor in the leadership of the fight against leprosy.

In 1936 the Council endorsed with pleasure a resolution of the New York Committee congratulating Mr. William Danner on the completion of twenty-five years' service as General Secretary of the American Mission to Lepers. Great success had attended Mr. Danner's efforts. In 1911 the income in the U.S.A. amounted to $15,000; in 1935 the figure was over $175,700. Mr. Danner retired soon after and was succeeded as General Secretary by the Rev. Emory Ross.

There were changes in the secretariat of two of the Mission's Auxiliaries. The names of the Rev. Charles Ellis as Secretary for Ireland appears for the first time in 1937. In 1940 Mr. F. C. Perry died, and in his place the Rev. F. A. Thompson was appointed secretary for New Zealand.

The Council of the Mission also suffered serious losses, the first and greatest of these by the death of the beloved founder of the Mission in his ninety-first year. No better tribute to his memory can be paid than by reproducing in full the special resolution of the Council passed by standing vote at its meeting on March 16th 1937:

The Council of the Mission to Lepers in placing on the records of the Society the death of Mr. Wellesley C. Bailey at his home in Edinburgh on Thursday, January 28th, of this year, desires to render thanksgiving to God for the devoted life and work of His servant. The Council rejoices that it was given to Mr. Bailey to labour for so many years on behalf of the lepers and also to see the remarkable development of the Christlike work he was led to initiate.

Mr. Bailey's sympathy for the lepers with whom he first came in contact in his early missionary service in the Punjab, India, and his desire to bring to them spiritual comfort and alleviation of their physical distress, led to the founding of the Mission to Lepers in the year 1874. He became the first General Secretary of the Society and later Superintendent, which office he held until his retirement in the year 1917. Under Mr. Bailey's leadership the Mission's work was extended from India to China and other countries, with growing and widespread support for its objects. Thus it became international in character. Mr. Bailey's gracious personality, his humble-mindedness, his strong but simple faith, his capacity for securing the co-operation of others in different parts of the world who became fellow-workers with him, and his readiness to give credit to all for the results obtained, caused him to be held in enduring respect and affection. The Council believe the work of the Mission to Lepers so commenced and continued must constitute a Memorial to Mr. Bailey whose name is inseparably associated with it.

Only a year later the President of the Mission, the Most Rev. Charles Frederick D'Arcy, D.D., Archbishop of Armagh and Primate of all Ireland, died at the age of 79. He had become President in 1920 and continued to hold this office until his death, maintaining a warm interest in the work and 'ever ready to advocate the cause of the lepers'. He was succeeded as head of the Church of Ireland by the most Rev. John Allen Fitzgerald Gregg, D.D., who honoured the Mission by accepting the office of President in succession to Dr. D'Arcy. A third loss was that of Sir William Fry, D.L., who died in August, 1939. He had been elected a member of the Committee of the Mission in 1914, and became a Vice-President six years later. He was the first Chairman of the newly constituted Mission Council (1921) and held office until 1937, when he asked to be relieved of this responsibility on account of his advanced age. He was also Honorary Treasurer of the Mission from 1925 to 1935. It was said of him 'He brought to the consideration of the Mission's affairs outstanding qualities, wise counsel, and a fervent loyalty to his Lord and Master'. Mr. Walter B. Sloan was elected Chairman of the Council in his place.

Between 1936 and 1940 budget estimates were accepted at figures ranging from £41,000 to £44,000, and numerous grants for repairs to buildings were made, together with new construction projects and new equipment of various kinds.

The Mission to Lepers Corporation was formed as a modernization of the older property-holding body, the Leper Mission Trust Association. Attention was given to the provision of retirement allowances or pensions to workers of various grades. In these critical years of the Gathering Storm, as Sir Winston Churchill described this period, the Council steadily strove to give added strength, both spiritual and material, to the whole enterprise at every level. But would the Spreading Tree in fact prove to be strong enough to stand against the tempest when it finally broke?

Chapter Seven
THE STORM BREAKS

IN THE RECORDS of the Council for the years 1939, 1940, and 1941, there is no direct reference to World War II; it seems to have been simply ignored. There are however two indirect references which deserve mention. The first appears in the Minutes of the Council meeting of October 3rd, 1939; it states that the Council agreed to the request of the Secretary for India that the fund which he held in India for use in case of emergency be raised from Rs. 1,000 to Rs. 5,000 (*i.e.*, from £75 sterling to £375) 'in view of the present conditions in Europe and possible delay in the mails'. That is cool enough in all conscience, but of course at that time the 'present conditions' were those of the so-called 'phoney war' when nothing seemed to be happening on the Western front, and British soldiers were singing an absurd song about hanging out the washing on the Siegfried Line.

The other obscure reference to war conditions is found just one year later, on October 8th, 1940, when it was agreed to increase by £1,000 the insurance cover for the headquarters of the Mission at No. 7 Bloomsbury Square 'in view of the present situation'. No explanation is given for that phrase, and we can only speculate what it was that the General Secretary had in mind when he drafted that Minute. But if it means what it seems to mean, and refers to the situation created by the bombing of London, then this must be William Anderson's all-time masterpiece of understatement.

The proof of this is found in the Minutes of the very next meeting of the Council, again by implication and not by direct statement. At the meeting of December 10th, 1940, the attendance of members of the Council set a record low in the long history of the Mission. There were only *four* persons present—Mr. W. B. Sloan in the chair, the Rev. E. S. Allwood, Mr. H. R. G. Durham, and the General Secretary. How they got to the meeting no-one now knows, but there they were, and all honour to them. They did a little routine business and then finally picked their way home; that night the City of London burned under a rain of incendiaries.

Turning over the records of the Mission, it is hard to realize how hard-pressed some of the Mission's staff were in these critical years. Nothing was said officially about this difficult time. Readers of the magazine in the British Isles would of course realize what was happening; it is not clear whether the friends of the Mission overseas understood the true situation.

Mrs Hayward, the widow of the Editorial Secretary, Mr. William Hayward, who as Miss S. H. Stripling was a member of the clerical staff at Headquarters for 15 years, recorded some impressions.

First about travel. The members of the office staff at Headquarters live in London suburbs and normally spend about two hours each day coming to Town and returning home. This daily journey was now more time-consuming, and even hazardous.

> Those who travelled by bus were often turned out *en route* when danger was imminent, got to the nearest shelter and then back to the bus to resume their journey. I remember on one occasion when the bus driver shouted, 'Duck!' Which we all did as a flying bomb skidded over the top of

the bus cracking windows in its flight—but we sat up and went on our way. Those who travelled by Underground had to step over the feet of already settled 'shelterers' on the way home at night, and of those (mostly children and old folk) who were still in position when we came back in the morning. Needless to say, the smell at times was awful!

The homes of the people of London suffered severely.

Most members of the staff had their homes damaged on more than one occasion, and of course, often had to cope without gas, water, or electricity. One member of the staff (Miss Hodgson) who had been completely bombed out of her home shortly before joining us, managed to find a small flat and get one or two items of furniture from friends, only to have that damaged by bombs two or three times. On one occasion she was blown across the room and had a necklace torn from her neck by the blast.

The office work itself suffered all kinds of hindrance and must often have been very difficult.

In the early days of World War II the staff resorted to the basement which housed the strongroom, the boiler, and the caretakers' flat, when the siren sounded. However, it was soon evident that this meant a waste of time, so we ultimately went down only when it was clear that danger was close at hand. From the earliest days of the war all records and typewriters were taken to the strongroom each night. Getting the magazines despatched was only one of the problems—especially as the printers moved out into the country after their premises were damaged—but Canadian and U.S.A. copies continued to be sent off from Bloomsbury Square. Wants parcels too were despatched whenever possible. These were mostly attended to by Mrs. Elliott in those days, with other volunteers, quite often on Saturday afternoons. Fuel was very scarce and it was often difficult to keep the place warm enough to work properly.

But the fellowship did not break down.

Mercifully no member of the staff was seriously hurt, and there was a splendid comradeship and helpful sharing of clothing coupons and even sweet coupons. Mrs. Hindes reminded me recently that I was able, through a relative, to get her the luxury of a new toothbrush at one time!

Finally, says Mrs. Hayward,

> You will doubtless have learned from others of the difficulties in keeping deputation work going, but it was wonderful how contributions to the work were maintained.

That last sentence reminds us that many of the cities and ports of Great Britain were heavily bombed, and the work of local secretaries of the Mission and helpers of all kinds must have been of a very high order to maintain a steady flow of support. The work went on nevertheless and the devotion of the workers was rewarded by equally devoted support. In 1944 the total ordinary income of the Mission, apart from legacies, reached a new record of more than £140,000, an increase of nearly £30,000 on the total for 1943. Britain could take it, and so by the grace of God could the Mission. It is a privilege to pay this small tribute to the courage and faithfulness which held firm against the fury of the storm.

Then came the second major threat, this time from an entirely different quarter. The ambition of the Japanese warlords was by no means satisfied with the attack on China already mentioned. They conceived a grandiose plan to conquer Asia, just as Hitler sought to be master over Europe. On December 7th, 1941, the Japanese made their devastating attack on the American fleet at Pearl Harbour, followed by a vast sweeping movement over South-East Asia until the Japanese forces stood at the very gate of India in the north-east corner of Assam, and a number of aided stations supported by the Mission and the American Mission to Lepers were engulfed in the flood of invasion.

It was in January 1942 that the Rev. C. H. Chapman wrote saying that he was taking precautions:

> Here in Mandalay we have our trenches dug, but so far have had only two alerts. Very many are leaving the city, but we intend to stay on—unless ordered away. We are anxious that you should not be too concerned about us out here. We are conscious that we are in God's hands and our way will be made clear, and, if we are to keep on, ways and means will be provided.

Only a short time later—on Good Friday, of all days in the year—Mandalay was heavily bombed and a great part of the town destroyed, with many buildings, constructed of the fine teakwood for which Burma was famous, burnt to the ground. On Easter Sunday morning, Mr. Chapman with a small group of friends sang the Easter hymn in the ruins of the Methodist Church in the town, and soon after all British personnel were ordered to leave Burma, together with any Burmese nationals who cared to accompany them. Moulmein had already been overwhelmed, and Rangoon taken by the Japanese, and there was therefore no sure escape by sea. So Mr. Chapman led a party of refugees on the long, weary trek north, finally turning west into Assam and then south to Calcutta. The story of that march itself a minor epic of endurance.

As the Japanese pushed further north through Upper Burma it looked as if some of the Mission's Homes in North India might have to be evacuated, and plans were made accordingly. Stations on or near the east coast of India were also seen to be at risk of attack by sea, and the Rev. E. R. Lazarus thought the Cuttack Home appeared to be vulnerable because of its position. Like Mr. Chapman before him, he took precautions:

> In view of the present situation, I had several slit trenches dug here and there at the Leper Home, chiefly under trees, but the men and women have been advised to take shelter if possible in their own rooms, in the corners of the same, and away from any draughty place. Some ships (merchant vessels) were sunk by enemy action in the Bay of Bengal, along the coast of Orissa. The men who were saved and came ashore and the wounded have been placed in our Cuttack General Hospital. Naturally, those who at the time did not know just what had happened had a scare. On the whole our patients are calm and are trusting in God. We are hoping for the best, but taking necessary precautions.

One may suppose that the Cuttack precautions would have proved as hopelessly inadequate as the Mandalay trenches did, if they had been subjected to the same fiery trial. However, it was not to be, and in fact only one Indian Home was overrun. This was the aided station at Kangpokpi in Assam, near the Kohima/Imphal area where the British and their allies made their final stand. Dr. Oliver Hasselblad, later the distinguished President of American Leprosy Missions, Inc., was in Assam from 1938 to 1945, and he confirms that leprosy work at Kangpokpi came to an end for a time.

At Kangpokpi the leprosy work and general medical work were forced to close. No foreign personnel were able to stay in Manipur after the Japanese invasion and until the Japanese were pushed back. Then our missionaries undertook a gigantic relief work in Manipur and restored the work. An interesting side-light was that the leprosarium was actually occupied by succeeding waves of Japanese and Allied forces as the battle ebbed and flowed. They were billeted in the patients' quarters and no-one seemed to mind. My first trip back there was in 1945. Every building in the leprosarium and the general medical compound, including bungalows, was riddled with shell fire. We had a tremendous task of rebuilding.

Dr. Hasselblad was the medical officer in charge of the work at Jorhat. This is his note on the situation there.

The Japanese pushed within about eleven miles of Jorhat but never in strength. In addition they did drop paratroopers close by on several occasions. Manipur and Dibrugarh had actual bombings but not enough to do much more than cause enormous panic and glut roads, rail and all kinds of communication. This was an obvious purpose, to cause chaos and despair. Thanks to the presence of the British, and later American, Australian, West African and other Allied forces, chaos was averted, and finally the Japanese were pushed back over the Manipur road and out of Assam.

The general situation in India was very tense for a long time. The fall of Singapore, a fortress believed to be impregnable, had a profound effect on the peoples of South-East Asia. It had been almost universally accepted that Great Britain and the United States of America were giants whose might could not be challenged, and here was an Asiatic power which had apparently destroyed the myth of the Western supermen. In India it seemed for a time that Britain was on the verge of complete defeat and anti-British subversive forces were soon at work. There was even an Indian National Army, as it was called, raised to fight side by side with the Japanese against the British. At the height of the crisis there appeared to be danger that at least a part of India would be lost, by subversion from within if not by attack from without, and with that loss the Mission might well have lost a part of its main field of activity. Only slowly and painfully was the tide of invasion first halted and then reversed, with the final result that all the world knows. In the meantime this part of the Spreading Tree had been severely tested.

Whatever the political situation was in India at this time, and however alarming the advance of the battle fronts might at one period have seemed to be, the Mission's ministry of healing went steadily on, and was even not without its encouraging moments. Here is the Rev. A. Stanley Jones, writing from Raniganj:

> We have been getting some cheering news of old patients. They write back to tell us of their progress in the world just as if they were writing back to their old school. Monilal, who was one of our scouts and the outside-left of one of the football teams, was discharged as symptom-free some little time ago. He is now in charge of a group of labourers at one of the aerodromes, and is doing very well indeed. Radha Gopal, another arrested case, is fulfilling the promise that he showed while still in the Home. We hear that he is making splendid progress at the High School, and that he stood second in the class at the last annual examination. Kulabala Sircar, another of our 'old scholars', is about to take her final examination as a nurse at the Jiagunj Hospital, and we have received happy reports about her and her work. Lekhjan Mondal wrote a short time ago and after expressing her gratitude for all that the Home had done for her, went on to tell us how well she is getting on at the weaving school connected with the Arakandi Mission Technical School. It is a great joy to hear all this good news of our old friends—or rather young friends, who were so recently our patients. It makes us realize that the Home is more than a place of healing for sick bodies, or of refuge for

those whom the disease has maimed. It is a school, a school of life, a place of culture for both mind and spirit, and those who have lived in this ashram and known its gracious influence go forth into the world with a healed body, but carrying the infection of a new life.

The Rev. Dr. D. A. McGavran made an interesting discovery at the Victoria Leper Home, Mungeli, one day in 1943.

One of our inmates, whose former name was Chamarin, had come in with 'ears and eyes extinguished' as she said, sick with leprosy, nearly deaf, more than half blind, down and out. An operation on her eyes helped, the injections brought back a measure of strength and with it of hearing. One day as I was chatting with her, I asked her about her antecedents, and found that she was a queen! At least in the Indian State of one hundred or so square miles in extent from which she came, she had at one time been called the Rani Saheba. She was in fact the wife of the younger brother of the ruling chief. 'My husband ran the State,' she said. 'He was much more clever in the affairs of the State than the Raja. Then he died. I became a widow, and then a leper. I wandered from place to place till you took me in.'

There were difficulties (not connected with the war) with the Bombay Government over the Kondhwa Home near Poona because of the insistence of the Government on the compulsory segregation of 'vagrant lepers'. This policy of compulsion was acceptable neither to the Mission nor to the co-operating Society, the Church of Scotland Foreign Mission, and both withdrew from the management of this Home, which was handed over to Government. Dr. J. K. Mukherji was appointed superintendent of the large Home at Naini in 1941, and two Indian doctors were honoured by the Government—Dr. Chandy of Faizabad by the award of the title Rao Sahib, and Dr. Manohar Masih of Almora with the Kaiser-i-Hind medal (bronze).

In 1943 the Council made a decision which was to have important consequences in following years. This was to agree to the Executive Committee's recommendation that the Mission co-operate in a new scheme for the establishment of a Christian Medical College at Vellore, and that Dr. R. G. Cochrane be invited to become the Medical Secretary of the Mission once more, in addition to his duties as a member of the professorial staff of the College. By the end of 1945 conditions generally had improved so much that the Council was already considering the re-opening of work at Moulmein and Mandalay in Burma, at Hangchow in China, and at Valbonne in France.

On April 8th 1943 Miss Mary Reed was called Home in her eighty-ninth year. Her story is well known to friends of the Mission through Miss MacKerchar's book about her, and need not be told again here. Also, many will have read *All My Mountains,* a booklet published in November 1943 in which Donald Miller described the visit which he and Mrs. Miller made to Miss Reed at Eastertide some time before her death. They talked of her past experience through more than fifty years of suffering and dedication to the work in a lovely but isolated place, and in the last half hour before the Millers resumed their journeyings the conversation turned, 'as it always did so easily in that little sunny sitting-room of Miss Reed's, to the things of the Spirit'.

Miss Reed gave us some wise words out of her rich experience, and her final emphasis was upon the need for our ability and readiness to receive God's gift of the Spirit. 'He does not give by measure,' she said. 'It is the measure of our readiness, our preparedness to receive His gifts that determines the extent of what we receive. His giving is without measure. It is we who limit His empowering of our lives.' I asked Miss Reed if she would choose our last hymn together. Although it was in the fresh morning light that we met together Miss Reed chose 'Abide with me', thinking of that eventide which is hers. It was strangely moving to sing these familiar words, as we thought of our own immediate departure, and Mary Reed left there alone in her outpost corner of the world.

> *I fear no foe with Thee at hand to bless,*
> *Ills have no weight, and tears no bitterness;*
> *Where is death's sting? where, grave thy victory?*
> *I triumph still, if Thou abide with me.*

In silence and in speech we prayed together, with hearts full, glad and grateful. And so we parted.

The then Secretary for India, the Rev. W. H. Russell, went to Chandag soon after Miss Reed's death to make arrangements for the continuance of the work, including the appointment of Dr. Katharine Young as resident medical officer and superintendent of the Chandag Home. One paragraph of his report to the Council was reprinted in the Mission's magazine of 1944 under the heading 'Banner Triumphant'.

Mr. Russell had said good-bye to the women patients, so broken physically, but so brave and radiant, and then went out to the narrow mountain pathway, where by the wayside he noticed a wild cherry tree.

'It had been cruelly broken by the storms which rage in the winter time, and was twisted and bent until it seemed that it was by a miracle that it survived at all. But there it was, still standing bravely in its place, and—wonderful to see—flinging out in a kind of gay defiance one last banner of courage, a single branch loaded with blossom which, gently drifting to the stony path beneath, laid a soft carpet of delicate petals for weary feet to tread upon. That tree reminds me of Harli of Chandag, a poor woman pitifully bent beneath her load of suffering, and yet still bearing bravely the banner of hope and love.'

Mr. Miller added his comment in one sentence:

That is a banner we all need to keep flying in these storm-swept days.

Then there was the death of Dr. G. B. Archer in tragic circumstances. He was a medical missionary of the Church Missionary Society who had actually come to the time of retirement, but gallantly offered to continue to serve as medical superintendent at Purulia. This is what Donald Miller said of him:

Of Dr. Archer it is most difficult to write because he was so close a personal friend, and because of the horror of the fact that he was shot by an unknown murderer in the dead of night, as he slept on the verandah of his bungalow. I knew no man more friendly to all, more hospitable, more humble in his walk with God. He came to Purulia after many years of distinguished medical missionary work in Bengal, and gave all his skill in the service of the leper folk. He soon came to love them, and later spoke of the years at Purulia as the happiest of his missionary service. After the Rev. E. B. Sharpe died in 1941 Dr. Archer shouldered the dual responsibility of general and medical superintendence, and made every aspect of the work in the Home his concern. Whether at prayer with his staff before the day's work, or in the pulpit, or in his surgeon's gown, or out in the gardens and fields encouraging the patients, or at home in the evening entertaining the many visitors who knew they would find a welcome, this fine Christian doctor was serving God with all his mind, and with all his soul, and all his strength.

In Purulia at the time the situation was very strained, and Wilfrid Russell hurried to Purulia to try to help Mr. Carswell in some very anxious and difficult days as he assumed general superintendence of the Home. The immediate need was to restore morale and offer encouragement to staff and patients alike in their bewilderment and sense of shock.

There was a crowded congregation in the Church of the Good Samaritan to offer thanksgiving for their beloved doctor's ministry, and to respond to a call to carry on the work of the Home and Hospital in the way Dr. Archer would himself have wished. There is at least one person who remembers the text the speaker used that day—Romans xii, 21: 'Be not overcome of evil, but overcome evil with good'.

China and Korea, hidden by war clouds, furnished little news in these six years. On the other hand the aided stations in Africa were not disturbed by the stresses experienced in India and the East. Of these most progress was being made at Uzuakoli in Nigeria, and in 1942 Dr. T. Frank Davey reported a successful and expanding programme.

The work of the Colony grows apace. We now have more than 6,000 patients in our care and are supervising no fewer than 29 out-station clinics. This year I shall be discharging at least 150 as symptom-free, and if staff permitted the work could be extended indefinitely. Our policy is not to diffuse our work over the Province, but to concentrate on one area where the leprosy incidence is very high. We are doing this, and 5,000 of our patients are from this area alone, although there probably remain another 10,000 within the area who are not yet in our care. These figures are staggering enough, but we are not dismayed, and you are giving us great assistance.

Bishop Chambers of Tanganyika describes a Confirmation Service at Makutupora in terms of peace and joy, very far removed from the sounds of battle:

Twenty-five lepers were confirmed. Dr. Wallace, who is in orders, gave his patients the Holy Communion afterwards, in which I assisted. 95 received the bread and wine of life at that Communion, pledges of the love of God to them. Truly a miracle has been achieved at Makutupora. God has indeed visited that place, and you, the Friends of Tanganyika, can share with me the deep joy for having brought fresh hope, life and the guarantee of a place in the eternal mansions, where they shall be clothed with bodies of glory.

Meanwhile there were few changes in the Auxiliaries. In the Council Minutes of 1943 'England' became for the first time 'England and Wales'. In the following year the Rev. Dr. W. Y. Turner became Secretary for Scotland in succession to Miss E. MacKerchar.

Dr. Eugene Kellersberger succeeded Dr. Emory Ross as General Secretary of the American Mission to Lepers in 1941. He brought to his new task practical experience of the work in the then Belgian Congo where he had been in charge of the colony at Bibanga. When the General Secretary of the Mission visited the U.S.A. towards the end of the war he joined Dr. Kellersberger and members of the American

Board in a comprehensive discussion of post-war planning of the work in China, India, and Africa. As long ago as 1945 Dr. Kellersberger questioned the use of the word 'Lepers' in the title of the Mission. In America there was said to be 'extreme sensitivity to the word and objection to its use', particularly at Carville, Louisiana.

In 1943 Mr. Walter B. Sloan, Chairman of the Council and a Vice-President of the Mission, died in his eighty-fifth year. He was widely known in evangelical circles in England and abroad, closely connected with the China Inland Mission and the Keswick Convention. In his place the Council elected as its Chairman a distinguished civil servant, Sir Walter Kinnear, K.B.E. At the meeting of the Council in December 1944 a new member was welcomed who has become very well known throughout the whole range of the Mission's activities—Mr. G. Newberry Fox. A year later, on December 10th 1945, the Council met for the hundredth time. One member present at the first meeting on 31st May 1921, was again present—the Hon. Mrs. Arthur Gordon. She was congratulated on her long membership of the Council.

At Headquarters Mr. William Hayward retired as Editorial Secretary on December 31st, 1945 after a long and devoted term of service stretching far back; it was in the reign of Queen Victoria and in the previous century that he joined the work. For 46 years, with only a short break during his military service in the first World War, William Hayward rendered valuable help in various departments, and for the last 26 years as Editorial Secretary. A newcomer to Headquarters staff appointed in 1945 was Mr. F. G. Torrie Attwell, later so well known to all as the Mission's very efficient Financial Secretary.

Two other interesting appointments were made by the Council about this time, each being the acceptance of an offer of missionary service. One would suppose that so marked a departure from the Mission's long-standing policy would have been preceded by considerable discussion, but there is no sign of this in the official record. Perhaps the first offer was so obviously attractive that it just had to be accepted!

It was made by a gifted young man named Laurie Baker, a qualified architect whose skill as a draughtsman and designer was to win great praise, and his service was gladly accepted by the Council in 1944. The next year Miss Mary Macdonald's offer was also accepted and she went to Purulia where she gave seven fruitful years of service. These offers seemed to come out of the blue, so to speak, and they raised questions of importance in the formation of post-war policy.

This summary of the events of 1939 to 1945 ends on a sad note. It was clear that the strain of the war years on the General Secretary was beginning to tell, and it is therefore no matter for surprise that in December 1941 Mr. Anderson reminded the Council that on June 30th 1942 he would have completed 30 years of direct service to the Mission and would then wish to retire. After due consideration at a special meeting the Executive Committee recommended that Mr. A. Donald Miller be invited to accept appointment as General Secretary in place of Mr. Anderson. The Council agreed, Mr. Miller was advised by cable, and at the next meeting of Council on March 18th, 1942, it was reported that he had accepted the invitation. On his advice the Rev. Wilfrid H. Russell was appointed Secretary for India on the basis of a five-year term of service. It was intended that Mr. Miller should return to London by the end of the year and take over the portfolio of General Secretary from Mr. Anderson, but it did not work out like that. William Anderson carried on in the expectation of Miller's arrival and remained in harness literally till the last moment, for on the 28th December, 1942 says Mrs. Anderson in her Memoir, 'he was hurrying to keep an appointment in the City with two members of the Council when he collapsed in the street not far from his office and passed away almost immediately'. Under the title 'An Ambassador for Christ' Donald Miller wrote a moving obituary. After reviewing Mr. Anderson's earlier career he went on to say:

And then, when the King's business brought this servant of Christ to the General Secretaryship of The Mission to Lepers 25 years ago, Mr. Anderson displayed those qualities of an ambassador which so fitted him for his special task. First an absolute loyalty to his King, then a deep sense of responsibility only to bear the King's tidings and none other, and finally a wide sympathy for and understanding of those to whom he was entrusted to be messenger and minister. In all his administration of the widespread work of the Mission, and in his contacts with the many countries from which the support of the Mission is gathered, Mr. Anderson displayed high qualities of Christian statesmanship and vision. And interfusing and illuminating these deeper characteristics were the graces of a thoughtful courtesy and a generous chivalry.

It was altogether appropriate, in spite of there being an immediate sense of tragedy for those who were left to mourn the loss of this knight of God, that Mr. Anderson should have been engaged in an errand of his Master when the trumpets blew and he was summoned swiftly into the presence of the King Himself. He had finished the course; he had kept the faith; and the crown of righteousness laid up for him was ready for bestowal.

Part Three

**THE SPREADING TREE
(1945 - 1960)**

Chapter Eight
HOW THE TREE BEGAN TO SPREAD

DONALD MILLER'S TRANSITION from being Secretary for India to the desk of the General Secretary in London was surely one of the most adventurous job changes any man has experienced. He and Mrs. Miller left India in 1942, to sail to England via the Cape in the S.S. *Cairo*. In the evening of November 6th, six days out from Cape Town, they were torpedoed, the liner sank, and passengers and crew took to the boats. Nearest land was the lonely island of St. Helena, 450 miles away.

In Mrs. Miller's pocket was the compass she had used for trekking with the girls at Purulia. With this to steer by, minimal rations to live on, and deep faith to sustain them, they and their companions in the boat endured thirteen days of sun, wind, and storm until the excited shout 'A ship! A ship!' spelt the end of the ordeal, a return to Cape Town and an eventual safe journey to England. The story is told in full in Donald Miller's remarkable little book, *A Ship! A Ship!* which has sold many thousands of copies, in 17 printings.

After brief visits to Donald Miller's home at Derby, where Mrs. Miller learned of her father's death in October, and to Mrs. Miller's home in Lincoln, the travellers came at last to London. As Mr. Miller has said, they had little more than the clothes they wore, as all the personal effects they had hoped to bring from India had gone down with the ship. Now they had to face the task of finding and equipping a home in London at a time when quite ordinary articles of household use and furniture were almost unobtainable. They needed clothes too; when Donald Miller finally took over his new work he was still wearing the grey flannel suit which he had had on when the ship was torpedoed.

Moreover, as Mr. Anderson had expected to hand over to Mr. Miller face-to-face, no preparations for the transfer had been made. There was not a note, not a single memorandum about any aspect of the Mission's affairs. He literally had to start from nothing, apart from his own experience of the work in India, and his own courage and fortitude. A formidable prospect, and the date was still only January 1943, when embattled London had much more to endure.

Even the welcome at No. 7 Bloomsbury Square, apart from Mr. Hayward's gracious gesture, was not exactly a warm one.

We went to Headquarters for me to take over the General Secretary's job on Thursday, the 21st January. Dear old Hayward greeted us and had managed to get a spray of carnations for Marjorie. At once I got down to settling in. When I was taken to the room so familiar to you, and which the General Secretary occupies, the electric light was switched on, as the long windows from floor to ceiling had been blown in, and the space had been filled in with hardboard with two little 'port-hole' windows to look through. Heating was at a minimum, and the linoleum floor (there was no carpet in those days) seemed to make it colder. However, I survived!

* * *

It has already been said that in this history of the Mission the facts will be allowed to speak for themselves, as far as possible and without too much in the way of comment. Only one person is capable of adequate comment, and that is Donald Miller himself. And this he does in the Postscript to *A Ship! A Ship!* in which he looks back on the ordeal from which he and his wife had been delivered.

For twenty years I had been engaged in the task of helping to provide havens of refuge and rescue for desperately needy men and women. I had seen them arrive in their tattered and soiled rags; looked into their careworn and ill-nourished faces; listened to their pitiful tales of separation from their loved ones and homes as the disease of leprosy had shattered their lives. But I had never known hunger and thirst myself; I had never known what it was to be cut off from human aid, and access to the world of men; I had never looked in vain upon bare horizons that offered no sign of hope or help. And I had never known what it meant at last, stripped and possessing nothing, to be taken into strong and welcoming arms, clothed and fed and made clean, and all without price, all with the sweetness and courtesies of gentle service.

But now I knew very much more of what these things meant. The material things of life took on a new value. While I learned on the one hand that so much is unnecessary, a mere weight and burden; on the other I also learned that much else is very necessary, if these earthly and yet heaven-bound lives of ours are to be lived as God intended them. And I saw that rescue ship of ours, coming to us when we were spent and stripped, as a symbol of what The Mission to Lepers, in its work of rescue, means to so many thousands of dispirited, diseased and lonely folk. I saw it more and more as a task of divine succour; at once sacramental and practical, making of the material service of human need a liberating act for the spirits of the children of God.

The period of Donald Miller's Secretaryship, 1945-1960, was one of sustained progress and growth. The factors contributing to this advance can be briefly summarized. First, and in many ways most important, was the opening of a new era in the treatment of leprosy by the introduction of the sulphone drugs on the one hand and the beginning of reconstructive surgery on the other. New interest was aroused at the Home Bases, resulting in a marked increase in the Mission's income, which in turn meant that as new opportunities for action presented themselves, resources were available to meet them. The General Secretary had at all times the confidence and support of the Council of the Mission under the direction of two able and devoted Chairmen. The most distant Auxiliaries were drawn closer to the centre and began to take an increasing share in discussions of general policy. New Auxiliaries were formed and important new projects on the Field were undertaken. The whole Mission was on the move.

Donald Miller brought to this challenging period in the life of the Mission the experience gained in his work as Secretary for India, and also notable gifts as speaker, writer, and artist, as well as administrator, and a certain flair for imaginative leadership at a time when just that quality was needed. In a word, he had charisma. This is a word the mass media have recently discovered and not always used appropriately. Here the word is used in the New Testament sense (*charisma* appears about twenty times in the Greek Testament) of God's free gift of spiritual life, grace (*charis*) and power. So among the various factors making for the advance of the Mission's work at this time we mention last but by no means least the fact that the administrative leader of the enterprise was in this deeper sense a gifted man.

In the chapter entitled 'The New Treatment' we have already noted Dr. Stanley Browne's comments on oil therapy, ending with the statement that an active drug was still awaited. This was a quotation from Dr. Browne's excellent little book *Leprosy: New Hope and Continuing Challenge*, published in 1966. We now quote again from the same source as Dr. Browne continues the story.

This active drug was lying unused on the shelves in the research chemists' laboratories. It was diamino-diphenyl-sulphone, a sulphone (DDS, or dapsone). It had been prepared by two German chemists as long ago as 1908; 30 years later it had been investigated simultaneously in London and in Paris and shown to be active in very small doses in experimental infections in mice. But further work showed the superiority of the large and growing group of chemical cousins of this drug, the sulphonamides, in combating infections in both animals and human beings.

In India DDS was tried out on leprosy by Dr. R. G. Cochrane, but it proved too toxic for human beings in the doses then employed. In the meantime the chemists prepared a number of compounds, some of which worked in leprosy, but their cost 'put them far beyond the reach of leprosy sufferers, save the very few'.

Then, something happened. Research workers found that these very expensive chemicals seemed to be partly broken down in the livers of leprosy patients into—believe it or not—the original diamino-diphenyl-sulphone, as well as small amounts of complex derivatives. Large doses of very expensive drugs seemed to exert their anti-leprosy action through tiny doses of very cheap dapsone. It was but a step (though it seemed to be a long succession of tentative and hesitant shuffles at the time) to giving small doses of dapsone by the mouth to leprosy patients to see if the same happy result could be achieved as with the large wasteful doses of the expensive compounds. Several people in different parts of the world, in late 1948 and in 1949, seemed to have the same idea—in Nigeria, in India, in French Indo-China, in Malaya, and in the Belgian Congo. By 1950 it was apparent that this was the road to follow, and the modern treatment of leprosy was established. In those days it was thought that a dose of two or perhaps three small (100 milligramme) tablets a day was necessary; now, it is established that one small tablet a week will give the same result, without the same risks of severe drug reactions, or dermatitis, or worse.

Dr. Browne comments that God must have been in this.

The cheapest, safest drug proves to be the best. And it still is, for the huge majority of those suffering today from the various types of leprosy. Given early, and with proper supervision, it is effective in well over 95% of all sufferers from leprosy.

The wide use of DDS as the standard treatment for leprosy soon began to show results, and it is not surprising that in some quarters dapsone was acclaimed as a 'miracle drug'. Dr. Browne deprecates the use of this term.

While the use of dapsone in the treatment of leprosy has revolutionized the whole outlook for leprosy sufferers, dapsone cannot be the final or best drug: we need something that acts more rapidly and more effectively.

He then goes on to discuss some of the problems remaining in chemo-therapy, and mentions new drugs such as Ciba 1906, diphenyl-thio-urea, first investigated by Dr. Frank Davey at Uzuakoli in Nigeria and by Dr. Ross Innes in East Africa, and a promising compound known as Lamprene (B663).

This safranin dye belongs to a group of about two hundred compounds synthesized in a Dublin laboratory by a research chemist, who was looking for a drug effective in tuberculosis. Minute traces of this powerful compound given in the diet of mice were found to protect against lethal doses of live tuberculosis bacilli. Since these bacilli are closely related to leprosy bacilli, it was suggested by Dr. Robert Cochrane that B663 might be active in leprosy. The first trials in Eastern Nigeria were very encouraging, and further trials have recently been inaugurated elsewhere. The staff at Uzuakoli were so impressed with the results that they told me that if ever they contracted leprosy they would ask to be given this drug.

The consequences of all this research were already evident in the medical work of the Mission well before 1960. The use of dapsone gave a new importance to the work of the physician and stimulated his enthusiasm. The fact that the drug could be given orally meant that a lot of the work involved in oil therapy could be eliminated, thus making treatment easier to handle both in the hospitals and in outpatient clinics. Indeed, this may well have been a factor in the wide spread of outpatient work which will be noted in the final decade of our study, 1960 to 1970. Another factor not to be overlooked is clearly brought out by Dr. Edwards of Moulmein, in his story about Maung Tin Shwe:

On May 25th, 1951, at 8 o'clock in the morning, a ragged little boy walked up to my desk and said, 'If you promise not to give me any injections I want to stay here.'

Dr. Edwards tells in detail the familiar tale of wandering here and there, this period ending with admission to a Leprosy Hospital in Rangoon.

Those were the days of painful intradermal hydnocarpus injections, an ordeal of treatment that even those with gross anaesthesia were loth to undergo. Overcome by terror, Tin Shwe one night ran away from the asylum, back to the graveyard from which he had come, where he fell in with a group of leprous beggars. For over two years he lived with those beggars. He was an asset to them, as his pitiable condition was a sure source of income. He was not ill treated, but all his earnings went to his protectors, who fed and clothed him as well as they did themselves—and drank and doped him to the same extent. Opium was the one drug they knew that would cure all their pains—the pain of neuritis, the ache of a tooth, the dull throbbing of a septic osteomyelitis; and it was always available at a price. But it was a raw deal for this boy, this life of begging, eating, drinking, gambling, quarrelling, and indulging in every vice as shamelessly as a normal person would indulge in harmless recreation.

One day in April 1951 Tin Shwe heard a visiting beggar from Moulmein discussing the Leprosy Home there with his protectors. This man said, among other things, that all patients in Moulmein were treated orally with a new drug (every patient in this Home was on oral DDS by February 12th, 1951).

So Tin Shwe came to Dr. Edwards, ready to enter the Moulmein Home if there were to be no injections!

He had been with us for a month when I sent for him and a batch of boys to have their haemoglobin checked. Boy after boy came and had his finger pricked. Tin Shwe held out till last, and then, in tears of terror, he cried, 'You promised me, no injections!' A second and third month passed, and each time the boy held me to my promise. The fourth month Tin Shwe came to me and hesitatingly held out his hand. 'Why?' I asked. 'This is not an injection,' he replied. Before leaving he looked at me and smiled: 'It doesn't really hurt!'

Not long ago, Ko Hla Maung, who teaches the Bible in school and is a Sunday School teacher, came to me with a list of eight names. They were, he told me, those who wanted to be baptized this year. There was a tightening round my heart as I looked at the name heading the list—MAUNG TIN SHWE.

In the next two decades there are stories of response to this new chemotherapy, almost always telling of improvement, and in some of the early cases quite dramatic change in the health and outlook of the patient. Oral therapy had come to stay.

In the meantime the Mission had recognized the need to provide medical leadership of higher quality. In addition to the recruitment of missionary doctors, which will be mentioned in the next chapter, medical scholarships continued to be given to selected Indian workers and these now covered training up to university standard, the M.B., B.S. degree of

Madras University or its equivalent. Two of these scholarship holders have since done distinguished work—Dr. C. K. Job and Dr. R. H. Thangaraj—and the former of these was enabled to gain the high qualification of M.D. in pathology, while both of them, together with Dr. (Mrs.) Thangaraj and Dr. Ernest Fritschi were accorded facilities for post-graduate study in Great Britain. At a different level similar help was provided for the training of laboratory technicians and other national workers of a similar grade by awards from the Anderson Memorial Scholarship Fund.

As its title suggests, the Anderson Memorial Fund was raised to honour the memory of the late General Secretary of the Mission, W. H. P. Anderson. There was a good response to an appeal for contributions, and the sum of a little over £5,800 was received in special gifts. One is glad to think that among other donors staffs and patients of many Homes in India sent their gifts. Part of the money was invested to form the Scholarship Fund referred to in the preceding paragraph, and the rest was used to erect a block of small wards for boys and girls with leprosy requiring hospital care of a temporary nature who previously had had to go into the adult hospital wards. This new memorial building, needless to say, was located at Chandkhuri, where Mr. Anderson had begun his long service with the Mission.

Mention of Chandkhuri and the children recalls the story of Tirlochan and his first impression of the Home. He was another wandering waif like Tin Shwe of Burma, though perhaps he did not sink to the same depths, and he did at least have the company of his elder brother, who also had leprosy. But their experience was in some respects the same, and they were driven from pillar to post until finally Tirlochan found his way to Chandkhuri at the age of eleven and asked for admission. Four years later he was said to be free from all signs of the disease, or nearly so, and there was hope that in another year or so he would be discharged as a healthy boy. Now he tells of his first impression of Chandkhuri:

> I can tell you, at first we were afraid. When we saw all the big buildings we really wondered if we had arrived at the

right place. We wondered how all this could be for lepers, including ourselves. Never, never, will I forget that day when we stood at your door and you came out and gave us a friendly smile. And, never will I forget when we were taken over to the Leper Boys' Home. We had nothing but rags on our bodies, and when new clothes were given us we could hardly believe our eyes. And then, that first plate of rice! I'll never forget it. For weeks we had not had a real meal.

A typical boy, remembering that first plate of rice! Then there was Mariam, a little Indian girl, who had cause to remember certain mangoes. We regret to say she was naughty, and was doing something which she knew was forbidden.

'Don't you dare to tell!' she warned her two little friends who stood below, as she scrambled up the tree (and just after Sunday School, too!) and out on to a branch where hung some fruit which was just getting ripe. 'You shall have some fruit if you don't say anything.' Mariam grabbed the mangoes quickly and started to come down, when she felt a stabbing pain in one toe. Giving her foot a shake, she looked to see what had hurt her—and saw two scorpions fall to the ground. 'Scorpion! Scorpion!' shrieked her friends, and catching up stones they battered the creatures to death, for they knew how dangerous they were. Meanwhile Mariam had got down from the tree and was showing her fruit and was giggling over her adventure. Suddenly the pain in her foot, from being a prick, became an agony that ran up her leg and seemed to set all her veins on fire. She fell to the ground moaning, while her friends rushed to get help. The doctor and a nurse came running, to find Mariam lying unconscious on the ground, and by the time they had carried her to hospital she was very near to death. Fortunately nowadays there are injections which can be given against scorpion bites, but for several hours doctor and nurses had to work hard to save the little girl's life. But Mariam did get better, and in seven days a rather weak and shaky little girl came out of hospital to rejoin her friends.

She had had a nasty shock, and we may be sure she remembered those mangoes, and those scorpions, for a long time. For a scorpion bite is indeed unforgettable.

Turning back to the theme of advance in medical terms, it is interesting to note that as part of this general advance the Mission now prepared to enter the field of research. Many years before Mr. Anderson told a conference of superintendents that research was not the Mission's business, and could safely be left to other agencies, while in 1948 Dr. Maxwell warned the Council about the cost of research. He said that his own experience in China had been that 'such work cost a great deal more than was originally estimated'. Even so, the Council agreed to discuss with its counterpart in New York Dr. R. G. Cochrane's proposal for a Research Unit in connection with the extension of leprosy work to be undertaken at or near Vellore (of which more below), and ten years later Council made a substantial grant towards the cost of equipment for pathological research directed by Dr. Job. In 1958, the Mission also gave support to the Register of Histopathology and Reference Laboratory (now called the Leprosy Study Centre) which Dr. Cochrane had by this time established in London. Right at the end of the fifties the Government of India inaugurated a comprehensive scheme for the establishment of centres for 'S.E.T.' (*i.e.*, Survey, Education, and Treatment). At the October meeting of 1960 the Council agreed to co-operate in this scheme and advised the superintendents of the Mission's hospitals accordingly.

While these things were happening in the field of medicine there was also an important development in the related field of surgery. In the records for the year 1952 appears for the first time the name of Mr. Paul W. Brand, M.B., F.R.C.S. The record does not explain how Dr. Brand came to be at Vellore, or how he came to be interested in leprosy, though we may reasonably suppose that Dr. Cochrane was mainly responsible.* All we are told is that Dr. Brand described his work at the Christian Medical College, Vellore, and urged the Council to make provision for workshops and simple accommodation for patients undergoing training in the

---

*See *Ten Fingers for God*, by Dorothy Clarke Wilson (Hodder and Stoughton).

proposed new research institution. In the next year (1953), he was invited to join the Mission staff, and agreed to do so. He is not only a brilliant surgeon; he also possesses the gift of lucid exposition to a marked degree, whether speaking of technicalities to a professional audience, or describing his work to a non-professional group of supporters of the Mission. Here is Dr. Brand talking to the Mission's Autumn Conference of 1952:

> These lepers have quite good hands and they have quite good minds, and they know what they want to do. Now when I want to do something the first thing I do is to think about it with my mind, and my mind says, I want to pick up that pen. And while I am thinking that a message goes down my nerves to my hand and my hand responds to that message and picks the pen up; and then my mind says, I want to put it down, and the message goes down to my muscles and I put it down. That is all there is to it. But we find that leprosy, when it gets into a man's body, seems to concentrate all its ferocity upon the nerves, upon the means of communication between the mind, which is still quite good, and the body which is still quite good; the mind thinks, I want to pick up that pen, and the arm gets as far as the pen; but the fingers do not know what to do. They have never heard the message 'pick up that pen', and they lie there idle and useless, because the nerves have gone. In the same way, if I put my hand under the hot water tap and the water happens to be too hot, instantly a message comes to my mind saying it is too hot, and before I know what I have done I have pulled my hand away. But the leper puts his hand into hot water, his hand is crying out 'too hot', but the message has never gone to the mind. The first thing a leper knows is that his hand is covered with blisters, these burns become septic, and he loses his fingers; not because his hand has leprosy but because his mind does not know what his hand is doing.

Dr. Brand then explained in an equally simple way what is really the basis of a series of operations he developed for the correction of the 'claw hand' so often found in leprosy.

> God has helped us to find one other fact, that in the hands of every leper there is remaining just one nerve that has not

been diseased. It is the nerve that runs down the very middle of the arm, and it gets as far as the wrist before the disease attacks it. And even there is one living, active nerve. We have not yet been able to find out how to restore function to nerves that have died; but we have been able to stretch the fibres of this one remaining nerve to help it affect the fingers and thumb, and we have had the joy of seeing the hand respond to the impulses of the mind, and become useful again.

Many friends of the Mission will have read of the remarkable successes achieved by Paul Brand and other surgeons trained in his techniques, or may have heard missionaries on furlough describe these things, or have seen films similar to the one described in chapter 10 of this book. They will also know of the fine work done by the great ally of the surgeon—the physiotherapist—in both pre-operative and post-operative treatments. All this is now almost common knowledge, and perhaps taken for granted to some extent. 20 years ago it was a wonderful new upsurge of life in the Spreading Tree.

Looking back at Paul Brand's pioneer work it seems the most natural thing in the world that two consequences should follow. One was that with such advocacy great interest should be aroused, particularly when Dr. Brand's famous film *Lifted Hands* became available for audiences in many countries. The other was that under such leadership the use of surgery in the service of the sufferer from leprosy should make rapid advance in the correction and prevention of deformity, in the provision of sheltered industries for people with disabilities, and in the whole field of rehabilitation.

There were, however, still those cases for whom the surgeon and the physiotherapist arrived too late; the damage had already been done. For instance there was the old woodcarver at the Happy Mount Leprosy Colony in Formosa who had for 20 years seen those clever hands of his slowly destroyed, until there were only stumps of fingers left. News had come that a great friend of the Mission was coming to Happy Mount, and the patients longed to show their gratitude by making him a gift, but what could they give that would be good enough? The old woodcarver had the knowledge—but could those broken hands of his get back enough of their skill for just one more task?

The lady superintendent bought him tools and a lovely block of camphor wood. Night after night the old carver lay awake, praying, 'God, give me back my skill. God, let me do it once more.' Then he set to work. But how hard it was to grip the tools with those poor stumps of fingers! Great was his joy when he found that, though he worked so slowly, the old skill was still there. The work began to take the shape he had seen in his mind before he started. When the tools slipped they did not gash the wood, though they often gashed his hands. Sometimes the pain was so bad that he had to rest for a day before he could go on. 'God, please let me finish it for him,' he prayed. And, winding more bandages round his hands, he took up the tools again.

The time for the visit drew near, but the woodcarver dared not try to hurry. One careless movement, and the whole work would be spoiled. Patiently he worked on, sending up a prayer with every stroke of his tools. At last it was finished—in time. His fellow patients gathered round to exclaim and admire the lovely thing he had made. It was a carving of a water buffalo, so perfect that it seemed to be alive, and the old man, nursing his aching hands, sent up a prayer of glad thankfulness to the Lord who had been a carpenter, Whose hands had been skilful with tools, and Who, the woodcarver was sure, had guided him in making his last offering.

Fortunately it was possible to take full advantage of the lead Paul Brand had given. As early as 1946 the American Mission to Lepers had agreed to make substantial capital funds available for the erection of a leprosy research unit for adults, which would be allied to the appropriate department of the Christian Medical College, Vellore, and which was finally built at a village called Karigiri, about ten miles from Vellore. (It was also originally intended that a children's sanatorium should be established as a parallel institution, but as no suitable site could be found at Vellore it was later built at Faizabad.)

This sanatorium for adults was to be named in honour of

The leprosy sufferer has needs at every level of life—body, mind and spirit. The Mission's ministry is directed to all of these, and shares the Gospel of Christ through literature (as here), pastoral care, and personal witness.

Health education can prevent altogether the damage to limbs which untreated leprosy often causes. In Korea the Mission's mobile team is equipped with its own generator so that films and slides can be projected in the most remote areas. The audience here is captivated by the medium and the message.

the first President of the American Mission to Lepers, Dr. William Jay Schieffelin, whose contacts with the Mission went as far back as 1906 and whose deep interest in the work continued until his death in 1955 at the age of 89. In 1952 the Mission received from America a grant of £20,000 for the erection of the new sanatorium, and in September of that year the founder of the Christian Medical College, Dr. Ida Scudder, broke the ground. The formal opening of the Schieffelin Leprosy Research Sanatorium took place on December 19th, 1953. Since then the institution has achieved wide renown and not only for its research activities; it has become a centre for training in reconstructive surgery and allied techniques, visited by trainees from all over the leprosy world. Its maintenance costs have been met, apart from Government grants, by American Leprosy Missions and The Leprosy Mission in roughly equal proportions.

Several other major projects undertaken between 1946 and 1960 will be mentioned in the next chapter. Here we complete the general survey of this period with a quick look at the Homes in India and Burma. Mandalay was reopened in May 1946, and the Council made grants for reconstruction and repairs. About the same time an account of the situation in Moulmein was received from a senior Chaplain to the Forces.

I found the property in a fair condition. The church had suffered somewhat in that almost all the tiles were blown off by a nearby bomb dropped in May last. All the pews and other furniture have disappeared, so it is quite bare. At present there are some 60-70 inmates. Most of them were living there before the Japanese entered this area in January 1942. At that time, however, they scattered to various parts of Burma. About 18 months or so ago they began to trickle back to what was their home. It is hard to discover how the poor things existed, but somehow they managed to eke out a living. They were in a shocking state when the British moved in here; they wore sackcloth, and some had died from malnutrition.

It was he who told of a patient whose condition deteriorated through lack of treatment during the Japanese occupation. (She died in 1951.)

An Anglo-Burman woman, who as a pretty girl in her second year at Judson College contracted the disease, has been the mainstay of things. She is a fine Christian and has done much for the others. Since I last saw her (in 1940) she had gone back, physically, a great deal. Treatment was holding the disease in check, but the lack of it has allowed it to ravage her, so much so that she can hardly walk now, and her fingers have thickened and warped so that her hands are almost useless. Her name is Marjorie Wilkins.

The other Sunday I was out at the asylum with a fine American Baptist Mission Biblewoman, Ma Hannah, the doctor, and two or three others, for a service. I think everyone came, looking almost as they would at Christmas, for they had recently been given new clothes by the Civil Affairs people who, by the way, are also giving them rations. How I wish that I could have taken a picture of them sitting in that roofless church, but even more I wish you could have heard Marjorie singing a very nice duet 'Jesus, Tender Shepherd' along with an Anglo-Burman lad. She has a very sweet and fairly strong voice. It was very pathetic.

The writer was Major the Rev. C. M. Lloyd. We shall hear of him again after his return to England.

The aided station at Raipur was handed over to Government and the small Homes at Jarhagaon and Meerut were closed, the patients transferred elsewhere and the property sold. The Mission later decided to withdraw from Cuttack, a Home owned by the Government, with the agreement of the Baptist Missionary Society, and from Raniganj, handing over the outpatient work at this station to the local Mines Board of Health.

The work lost two fine leaders by death, Dr. W. F. Joseph, of Calicut, and Dr. J. K. Mukherji, of Naini. Otherwise the story is almost entirely one of advance, with modernization of old buildings at Purulia, following a visit by Sir Paul Benthall, at Kothara and at Naini, the opening of the Mary Reed Memorial Hospital at Chandag, a new hospital block at Vadathorasalur, a new church at Poladpur with a fine tower designed by Mr. Laurie Baker, a new hospital at Moulmein (the funds raised locally by the superintendent, Miss Shivers), and plans for a new medical building at Bankura and a hospital chapel at Karigiri. Mention of the last item recalls a speaker at one of the Annual Meetings in London who talked about the names of the three places of worship in the Purulia compound—the children's chapel called 'The Chapel of the Kingdom', the hospital chapel called 'The Chapel of the Living Water' (so named in memory of the Rev. E. B. Sharpe's son, who was drowned), and the large church called 'The Church of the Good Samaritan'.

When Donald Miller and Ernest Sharpe (if it was these two in combination) hit upon this great name for the Church at Purulia, they brought in another thought, and a greater thought. It is true that the Good Samaritan performs the work of rescue; it is true also that the Good Samaritan performs the work of restoration and rebuilding; but this place is called the *Church* of the Good Samaritan. The *Church*! Not first-aid post; not casualty clearing station as they might have said in the war, though The Mission to Lepers does that work too: not for healing only, but the *Church* of the Good Samaritan. For, as you know when we seek to care for the bodies and minds of our people we speak to them also of greater things even than these. We bring to them the Gospel of the Lord Jesus Christ who died for them, as He died for us, and we speak to them of the grace of that same Lord Jesus Christ, and the love of God, and the fellowship of the Holy Spirit. And by His mercy there comes to them grace and peace.

Chandkhuri celebrated its Golden Jubilee and Kalimpong had a very distinguished visitor.

The first man to receive Lady Mountbatten at the Leper Hospital bowed deeply over his clasped hands in greeting. But she seized his hands in hers and shook them warmly. And so she passed along the lines, affectionately clasping the deformed and mutilated hands of every patient. It was a great gesture born of a great heart and loving imagination and the patients were very moved. Nothing escaped her notice. An ex-Gurkha was wearing the ribbon of the Burma Star. Excitedly she asked him, 'Who was your leader?' He drew himself up to answer, 'Lord Mountbatten'. More, as she was now greeting him, so had her husband once greeted him in the jungles of Burma. She visited the homes of the women and children and watched the school at work. She left behind in every heart a note of encouragement and new hope.

Purulia endured the ravages of a cyclone and Tarn Taran suffered damage from floods. (The Mission magazine of 1956 carried a fascinating picture of the intrepid Mrs. Das—the mother of Dr. Victor P. Das—sailing round the flooded Home in a bath tub!) There was no lack of incident in this period. The Tree spreads ever wider and it is no longer possible to count every leaf and twig.

Chapter Nine
ON TOUR

LIKE HIS PREDECESSOR, Donald Miller made a number of visits overseas to get to know the current situation at firsthand. These secretarial tours were very productive, and in this chapter an attempt will be made to assess some of the results which followed.

The first journey began in October 1947 and ended in April 1948, taking in India, Burma, and China. The tour is extremely well documented, for there is on record not only a full report to the Council but also a most attractive account of Miller's adventures published in 1949 under the title *Red Earth and Summer Lilies*.

Mr. and Mrs. Miller went by ship to India and together visited a number of stations. The General Secretary held several regional conferences in what had now become the usual way, and attended the first all-India Leprosy Workers' Conference at Wardha; he was able to meet in helpful discussion Government and other leprosy workers who were outside the Mission circle, but who were with the Mission in the same campaign against leprosy. From India Donald Miller went on to China, leaving Mrs. Miller behind in India to make the film *Purulia Pilgrimage*. In China he was joined by Dr. Eugene Kellersberger, General Secretary of the American Mission to Lepers. The two secretaries engaged in a long tour of about five thousand miles within China, ably planned by Dr. Neil D. Fraser, appointed Medical Secretary for China in 1946, and for the most part in his company. On the way back from Hong Kong Mr. Miller saw the two centres in Burma—Mandalay and Moulmein—before rejoining his wife in India.

We cannot but note the strenuous nature of a long six-months tour of this kind, involving at times quite arduous journeys and two or three changes of climate. To go to India in October is to go there at the best time of the year for touring, as the weather is then generally pleasant. But to go on to China in the winter, and especially to parts of that country high above sea level, is to ask for trouble. Donald Miller certainly got it. He was snow-bound in Lanchow for nine days, and when he did get away by plane it was by no means a holiday jaunt. ('We came down steeply at Chenchow to avoid the possibility of being shot at by surrounding Communists!') Moreover, Mr. Miller had attacks of malaria at Sining and Nanking, and was in need of those 'journeying mercies' so often mentioned in our prayers for one another.

The Millers were in India at the time of the assassination of Mahatma Gandhi, and noted the shattering effect of this tragic event on the people of India. He himself had met Mr. Gandhi, and had experienced the impact of this remarkable personality. Perhaps for this reason he shared the sense of personal loss expressed all over India at the time. Certainly there was a great loss to the anti-leprosy cause in which the Mahatma had set a notable example to his fellow-countrymen by his personal service to sufferers from leprosy.

Donald Miller reached Burma on the 11th of January, 1948, when the newly-formed Republic was just a week old; this was his first impression of Rangoon:

> I drove into the city eager to see how it was displaying its joy at its new freedom. I was ready to 'rejoice with

them that do rejoice'. But I was soon to mark the listlessness, almost apathy, which was the characteristic note of the city's life. One expected to find the ruins of bombed buildings. I was familiar enough with that in Britain. Even the roads along which one bounced, although badly out of repair, were understandable. But there was a deeper damage than that. There was a damage of spirit which still persisted. The old happy atmosphere was gone. Burma was paying the penalty of years of war, during which she had not only been invaded, but had suffered the scorched-earth policy both of the retreating British and then of the retreating Japanese. Her prolonged physical ordeal had done something to her soul.

Further evidence of the devastation caused by war was revealed in the journey to Moulmein and at the Home itself. There was encouragement in the story of Marjorie Wilkins, to which reference has already been made, and in a more hopeful outlook at Mandalay in spite of the fact that the centre of the town had been practically destroyed. But the real shock came in North China, and Chapter Eight of *Red Earth and Summer Lilies* is actually headed 'Drawn Bayonets in the North'. At Tsinan Mr. Miller and Dr. Kellersberger found themselves in a city prepared for siege and already surrounded by Communist forces. The Home at Tengshien was not visited; during the year the Home had repeatedly passed in and out of the Communist lines. The position at Tsingchowfu was equally obscure. Mr. Miller and his companions were in fact dangerously close to a movement that in a short time would sweep and over-run the whole country, finally driving General Chiang Kai-shek and his followers out and creating a new China. Dr. Fraser prepared an excellent memorandum on Medical Policy for China which was attached to the official reports to London and New York. Unfortunately, this is now of little more than academic interest, as indeed is the whole report on China, for within a very few years everything the Secretaries recorded so faithfully had been swept away. The Spreading Tree had lost one of its main branches.

The curtain now falls upon the China scene, apart from occasional glimpses from Hong Kong, but for the sake of the record we now reproduce one of the last messages from a China station, Chengtu, dated 1948:

On June 30th of this year we have forty-eight patients in residence, says Dr. Wallace Crawford. We have taken in two women, and made use of rooms for women which we had never thought of for such use. But six months of residence with us has made a real change in the lives of these two women. One is a wife of an army officer who contracted the disease while in an outpost with her husband. He has had to report back for duty in the West but she has remained with us, and her general condition has greatly improved. The other woman, a girl of eighteen who looks like forty, was brought in by her brother. When he came to us he weighed one hundred and twenty-eight pounds. Last Friday he weighed one hundred and sixty-eight pounds and he looks his improvement. He has also become a Christian and his smile and winning manner have won him a place among the patients. The sister was in a deplorable state, with scabies, ulcers, trophic ulcers, and malnutrition. She has blossomed out and while she will never be a beauty to look upon, her general condition has shown remarkable improvement. These two, brother and sister, are outstanding examples of what nutritious diet will do for sufferers from leprosy.

One wonders what happened to Dr. Crawford's two patients.

Still another subject came to the General Secretary's notice during his visits to Homes in India. Already plans for post-war development and expansion were forming in his mind, and some of them are recommended to the Council in his tour report. But he also noticed the changing relation between the Mission and the co-operating Societies, and the effect this was likely to have on missionary staffing. Some of these Societies were finding it difficult to maintain a full staff of missionaries on the field, and this meant that in some cases the Mission would have to supply the missionary personnel formerly provided by the co-operating Society. This actually happened at the Mission's largest Home in India, at Purulia, and in 1950 the Church Missionary Society withdrew from the leprosy work its missionaries had directed for many years.

Mr. Miller also saw that new work might be called for in areas where there was no Missionary Society capable of offering its missionary personnel in effective co-operation. The subsequent history of the Mission clearly shows that in adopting this new policy the Council was following the leading of the Spirit. It is true that there were a few disappointments, as Mr. Miller had feared, and some missionaries withdrew after a comparatively short period of service. Several young ladies got married, naturally with the good wishes of the Council. Miss Mary Macdonald withdrew in 1952, Miss Ruth Thomas married Mr. Kin Thein in 1957 and together they formed a splendid working partnership at Mandalay, Mr. Wilfred Bradshaw and Miss Rachael Bennett left the work at Hay Ling Chau for personal reasons, and in 1957 Mr. F. C. Carswell retired after seventeen years of service which included some difficult years at Naini and the Purulia tragedy already referred to in Chapter 7. Much earlier Mr. Laurie Baker was released from Mission employ at his own request. He married Dr. Chandy's sister, who was also a doctor, and for some years they carried on independent medical work not far from Chandag, though Mr. Baker continued to help the Mission with professional advice and plans for several new schemes. Dr. Katharine Young also resigned to take up independent work in a remote area north of Chandag. By and large the decision to adopt a policy of wider recruitment of missionary personnel was a wise one. It was also very successful in the contribution thus made both to leadership overseas and also to advocacy at home, for as time passed and missionaries began to take furlough, they told convincingly the story of their work to appreciative audiences in Great Britain and beyond, and so greatly increased interest in the Spreading Tree.

This judgement will surely be confirmed as we note the names of some of the missionaries appointed by the Council during the years 1950 to 1960:

In 1950: Mr. A. D. Askew, Mr. P. A. Brambleby, Miss Marian A. Rees.
In 1951: Mr. Ian G. Hayes, Dr. R. G. Riedel.
In 1952: Dr. Frances E. Bramwell, Miss Beatrice McKay.
In 1955: Dr. Hectorina Matheson (Mrs. Waudby), Miss M. W. J. Evans, Dr. L. J. Harman.
In 1956: Dr. J. C. Pedley, Mr. David J. Ward, Miss Beryl C. Batstone.
In 1957: Dr. Ian H. Cochrane.
In 1958: Dr. Grace Warren, Dr. C. Stewart Goodwin, Dr. Gerald K. Wilson, the Rev. James Waddell.
In 1959: Mr. Alan D. Waudby, Miss Jean Watson, Miss D. M. Banks (recommended by the Australian Auxiliary).
In 1960: Miss Joyce Ledger, Miss Claire Thistlethwaite.

It is an impressive list, many of them still with the Mission at the end of 1970, and through their service there has been great gain to the Mission's cause. How indeed could it have advanced as it did without the energy, skill, and devotion of these consecrated men and women?

There were also offers of service from medical men already distinguished in their profession. There was the generous gesture of Dr. Ernest Muir, when he went to India in 1949 to give two years to direct the medical work at Purulia, which was without a doctor at the time. Even more gallant was an offer made by Dr. James L. Maxwell, C.B.E., M.D., a member of the Council and a Vice-President of the Mission, and Mrs. Maxwell, to return to Hangchow until a vacancy there could be filled. But before Dr. Maxwell could be relieved by a younger man he was called to higher service on August 10th, 1951. The General Secretary paid an eloquent tribute:

It was in the last two-and-a-half years of his life that Dr. Maxwell rendered his most notable service to the Mission. I well recall the autumn day in 1948 when Dr. and Mrs. Maxwell came into the room in which I now write and, with the utmost simplicity, volunteered to go back together as unpaid helpers in order that our work at Hangchow, and the new project associated with it at Zang-peh, should not be hindered by the break-down in health of a European doctor, and our failure to secure a young successor to him.

Both were already in the middle seventies, and they had established a home in Bedfordshire, where Dr. Maxwell had a good practice. Moreover the whole political and military situation in China was complex and the future unpredictable. The upshot was that after both had been found medically fit, and the difficulties and risks had been fully discussed, the Council gratefully accepted the offer. 'If I should die in China', Dr. Maxwell said to me, 'then where better? That is the land and people it has been our privilege to serve.'

Nor should we forget the highly skilled service given free of charge over a period of two years by an orthopaedic surgeon in retirement after a distinguished career in the Australian Public Health Department, Dr. W. S. Robertson, O.B.E., M.B., Ch.B., F.R.A.C.S.

Dr. Maxwell's name is honoured by a Memorial Hospital built at a place he had never heard of, for all his wide knowledge of China, for the name of this place had not been invented at the time of his death. Not only were General Chiang Kai-shek and his followers swept out of China; the missionaries went too, and a number of them retreated to the British Crown Colony of Hong Kong. Among them was Dr. Neil Fraser, who had accompanied Mr. Miller and Dr. Kellersberger on their secretarial tour. His interest in leprosy work was now transferred to the leprosy situation in Hong Kong, and very soon the Council began to hear of a new project for the establishment of a modern leprosarium on a small island off Hong Kong, known at that time as Nun Island. This island was practically uninhabitable on account of a shortage of water, but a spring was found, and with the expert assistance of a party of Royal Engineers an adequate water supply was finally assured. So came into being the fine institution called Hay Ling Chau, the Isle of Hapy Healing. Here it was that the Maxwell Memorial Medical Centre was built, and in 1954 formally opened by H.E. Sir Alexander Grantham, Governor of Hong Kong. It was largely Dr. Fraser's drive and enthusiasm, and his wide experience of leprosy work, that created Hay Ling Chau, and built it up into an efficient centre caring for some 500 patients, set in surroundings of great beauty. He was ably assisted in the medical work first by Dr. L. J. Harman and later by Dr. Grace Warren and in administration by Miss Rachael Bennett and the Rev. James Waddell, who became administrative superintendent of Hay Ling Chau in 1958.

There was also strong support from the Mission's Hong Kong Auxiliary, established in 1950, which through the years raised large sums of money for the normal maintenance of the work and for new buildings and equipment. The Hong Kong Government made generous grants for the initial expenditure on the first set of buildings and for recurring maintenance costs, with the net result that the Mission's financial responsibility was largely confined to providing and supporting missionary personnel.

This was an excellent example of a project well planned, well executed, and well supported both by Government and the general public, and it offset to some extent the grievous separation from the work in China. It was also an instructive example of the way in which an Auxiliary can cope with leprosy at its very door, and confirmed the need for direct recruitment of missionary personnel by the Mission, for though there was a strong Christian community in Hong Kong which was sympathetic and most helpful, there was no Missionary Society which could offer anyone competent to take charge of so ambitious a project.

Every visitor to Hay Ling Chau has been struck by the beauty of the island, which has already been mentioned. But to many who came there as patients, and not as visitors, it must have seemed a veritable Paradise. Evidently May-Ling thought so; it is Miss Rachael Bennett who tells her story:

> This young girl had had a hard life. When she was only four she was engaged to be married to the son of a neighbour! This was because her parents were very poor, and it was one way, they thought, of providing for their daughter. As soon as she was old enough to do a little work in the house she was sent to her future husband's family, where she was like a little slave. She had to fetch wood, carry water, cook, sweep, and run errands all day

long; but she always hoped for the time when she would be married and she would have the joy of her own babies. That was not to be. She developed leprosy, and the family turned her out.

After a period of wandering she found her way to a leprosy home in the south of China, but soon came the news that the Communists were advancing from the north, and everybody was frightened, for they did not know what might happen to them. Many patients ran away, and among them May-Ling. She made up her mind that she would try to get to Hong Kong, where the British were in charge.

It was a long way to go, two hundred miles, and she had no money, so she had to go on foot and beg her way as she went, and also ask people to show her the right road. She never asked young people to help her, for she said afterwards, 'Young people are so unkind to people with leprosy'. But the old people were kinder.

At last after about a month's journey, she reached Hong Kong. She found it terribly bewildering in the big city. She had heard that there was a leprosy home somewhere, but she was afraid to ask. She knew no-one, and had nowhere to sleep, so she wandered about until she found an empty verandah and curled up there for the night. When she woke in the morning there was a strange, brown-faced gentleman standing over her. He was an Indian, but he spoke Chinese and he asked her very kindly all about herself. When she told him, he said that his friend was the doctor in the leprosy home! So May-Ling was taken by this kind friend to Hay Ling Chau, The Isle of Happy Healing, and how amazed she was to find herself in this lovely place, among kind, happy people, where she could be treated for her disease, and feel that she was welcome and useful. Now she realized that God had been guiding her all through her troubles, and she gave her heart to Him and became one of His disciples.

So far in this chapter we have dealt with only one of Mr. Miller's tours and developments from it. A similar result would follow from detailed study of the next tour, which covered the period October 1953 to the beginning of April 1954 in a visit to India and the Far East, and home via the U.S.A. and Canada, altogether visiting ten different countries. Then there was the Africa journey, the first visit paid by any General Secretary of the Mission to leprosy work in that continent. It took place at the end of 1955 and the beginning of 1956 and included visits to more than 20 centres. It is impossible to cover such a mass of material in a book of this kind, and fortunately it is not necessary because his experiences on these two tours formed the basis of another of Mr. Miller's books, *A Bridge of Compassion*. We will do no more than note some of the highlights.

Visits to the work in India call for little comment here, except perhaps to note the growing importance of the Indian Committee of Advice, the development of orthopaedic work, and an interesting suggestion that a team should visit Nepal and assess the leprosy situation there. This arose from the fact that both at Chandag in the West and at Kalimpong in the East patients were coming from Nepal after travelling long distances, thus indicating the need for leprosy work in their country. A Commission consisting of the Secretary for India, Mr. William Bailey, Mr. P. A. Brambleby, Dr. P. J. Chandy, Dr. V. P. Das, and Dr. Manohar Masih, of Almora, duly investigated conditions in Nepal and reported in 1955. By 1957 the Council had laid down the main lines of the Mission policy for Nepal based on the Commission's report, had agreed to co-operate with the United Mission to Nepal and had sent Dr. P. J. Chandy and Dr. J. C. Pedley to make a start with 'the nearest tasks'. A site was offered about ten miles from Kathmandu and a full scale programme was outlined.

Mr. and Mrs. Miller passed through Malaya to Hong Kong, where they were greatly impressed by everything they saw at Hay Ling Chau: the fine buildings, the evident interest displayed by the Hong Kong community, the generous financial support provided by the Government and the Auxiliary, and the 'driving heart of all this activity'—Dr. Neil Fraser himself. During the General Secretary's visit the Maxwell Memorial Medical Centre was formally opened. Mrs. Miller made a film during her stay on the island which appeared later as *The Story of Chengsu*.

After a brief call at the Happy Mount Colony in Formosa Mr. Miller went on to Korea. Here there was snow on the ground and a piercing cold wind. Moreover he found that the destruction caused by the recent Korean war 'had bitten deep into Korea'. The general position was bewildering, but he made some specific requests including one for 10,000 DDS tablets, unobtainable in Korea at the time. After some rather hectic telephoning this was promptly arranged through the head office of Imperial Chemical Industries. It was felt that the medical situation in Korea urgently needed investigation by Dr. Fraser and Dr. R. G. Cochrane, who might then advise how the Mission and American Leprosy Missions could best help.

For some time following his visit to Korea the General Secretary had this country much in his mind. Money was made available for Korea, and in 1955 the Mission decided to send out a team of workers in response to Dr. Fraser's strong recommendation. The Mission was to undertake an entirely new type of work in Korea—namely, to get out into the villages and establish a chain of clinics. An offer to take part in this new project was generously made by the Rev. C. M. Lloyd. After his service as a military chaplain during World War II he had returned home and had joined the Mission's staff as an Area Secretary in the North of England. The Council gratefully accepted Mr. Lloyd's offer, and he went out to Korea as leader of the team, accompanied by his wife and Miss Grace Bennett, later joined by Dr. Gerald Wilson and others. At the beginning there were many difficulties. Mr. Lloyd had no proper centre from which to operate, and little equipment and transport. He had to win local goodwill and establish some kind of headquarters in Taegu (in rented accommodation) with a number of village clinics housed in simple buildings. Progress was slow at first, but little by little the value of the new approach to the leprosy problem in Korea began to be recognized. By 1960 Mr. Lloyd, now on furlough, was able to report to the Council that since his arrival in Korea 12 village clinics had been established with a thousand patients on the register and an average monthly attendance of 500 to 600. In addition, contact had been made with about 40 colonies or groups of leprosy sufferers, not in regular institutions, while a four-bed unit had been erected in the compound of the Taegu Medical College. The good work of the Mission had also been officially recognized, and the magazine for 1958 had carried an article entitled 'The Republic of Korea says, "Thank you" ', from which this extract is taken:

> During June Mr. Lloyd had received an invitation to visit the National Leprosarium of Ae Sang Won on the occasion of the visit of the Bureau Chief of the Ministry of Health in Seoul. At this leprosarium, where over a thousand patients are accommodated, Miss Bennett has given visiting help at an eye clinic, and Mr. and Mrs. Lloyd have given help on the religious and social side. A hint was given that some sort of a presentation was to be made; but what followed was evidence of gratitude for the wider work engaged in by the Mission to Lepers team beyond Ae Sang Won. 'On arriving at the Leprosarium,' writes Mr. Lloyd, 'we were surprised to see a banner hanging across the entrance gate bearing the inscription, "Thanks Mission to Lepers". Our presentation, the only one, was made by Dr. Lee on behalf of the Minister of Health in the presence of a large group of the patients. I enclose herewith a copy of the "Letter of Appreciation". The original is in Korean and English in a lacquer case and blue silk cover tied with a red ribbon. While some personal gratification is permissible, we three feel that this is the least important aspect of the presentation. We are definitely of the opinion that this is a sincere and genuine expression from the Government that they like what The Mission to Lepers has done and they rejoice that we will not only maintain these activities, but extend them . . . During the short speech he made Dr. Lee made special mention of our having combined the spiritual with a practical approach.'

Much still remained to be done. It was clear that the Mission team could not continue indefinitely to operate from rented accommodation, and in 1959 a site was purchased for the erection of the Mission Centre on land about three miles outside Taegu. There was also a proposal to provide more adequate medical facilities than the four-bed unit could offer. These developments came later.

The visit to Africa was, as we have said, the first such tour of a General Secretary in that continent. American Leprosy Missions had a greater commitment in Africa, and its secretaries in recent years had been missionaries with African experience. The Mission had much less knowledge of African conditions, its General Secretaries having been drawn from the Asian field. It was therefore thought desirable to 'secure a general view of the leprosy work in the various countries visited' in Africa, and also a pictorial record on film which Mrs. Miller was asked to make.

Eight centres in Nigeria were visited, two of which call for comment here. The first was Uzuakoli, where Dr. Frank Davey was now in charge of the fine and very extensive work established by his predecessor. 'The services of Dr. John Lowe as Leprosy Research Worker in introducing on a wide scale the basic sulphone by oral administration were notable and remembered with gratitude'. Dr. Davey was carrying forward the same policy with energy and success. At Itu, a large institution with about 2000 patients managed by the Church of Scotland Foreign Mission, Mr. Miller had the privilege of attending a 'Discharge Announcement Ceremony' at which no fewer than 286 names (of patients ready for discharge) were read 'to the accompaniment of vociferous applause'. Then followed a thanksgiving service in the large church, built to hold about 3000, and a visit to Dr. A. B. Macdonald's palm-oil tree plantation from which the colony was said to be deriving an income of about £14,000 per annum! It is sad to think that this great work, declared to be perhaps the finest piece of organized leprosy work of its time, was later to suffer so severely in the Nigerian Civil War.

There was also trouble ahead for Congo Belge, as it was then called, but of course this was not apparent at the time. What was plain to see was the prosperity of the country and the considerable funds given by the Belgian Government for leprosy work. At Kimpese Donald Miller noted the need for a physiotherapist, and at Yalisombo he found in charge Dr. Stanley Browne, a highly qualified leader (both F.R.C.P. and F.R.C.S.) in the leprosy campaign who later became the Mission's Medical Consultant.

In Uganda the General Secretary heard of another extensive piece of work organized by the Government Leprologist, Dr. J. Kinnear Brown, comprising fifty treatment villages with between 20,000 and 25,000 patients. The work built up by Dr. Wiggins and Miss Margaret Laing of the Church Missionary Society at Kumi/Ongino was visited, together with Kuluva, 'a piece of missionary work of the storybook kind'—and an effective as well as a romantic story, the whole work managed by the famous 'Kuluva Family Williams'. Miller then went on to Lake Bunyonyi—'Lake of Little Birds'—where the Silver Jubilee of this Home was celebrated during his visit.

From the point of view of action resulting from the tour the most important visit was that to Makutupora in Central Tanganyika. There had always been a serious shortage of water at this institution, and the Government proposed a new central leprosarium to replace it. This scheme was discussed on the spot with the Bishop of Tanganyika, and out of this consultation there finally emerged the plan to build a new hospital at Hombolo. By 1959 a site had been secured, and in the following year Dr. H. W. Hannah, the son of the founder of the Mission's Australian Auxiliary, and himself a member of the Australian Church Missionary Society, had the pleasure of describing this site at the March meeting of the Council. He was told that the Council had set aside the sum of £5,000 for memorial buildings at Hombolo to honour his father's memory. So the Mission established this first piece of direct work in Africa.

From Tanganyika the Millers moved on to Kenya where the Mission had made a substantial grant for a new church building at Itesio, and then to the two stations in Ethiopia aided by the Mission, Dessie and Shashemane. Donald Miller ended his report on these two stations with a prophetic word: 'The hour has struck, I believe, for advance in Ethiopia leprosy work'.

The visit to stations in Africa stimulated interest in that part of the world which is reflected in the Mission's magazine by a number of stories. The most outstanding of these is the story of Salakwanda Zulu.

> On a bed outside the window of a small hospital ward in the Mbuluzi Leprosy Colony, Swaziland, lies a patient who cannot see the flowers on the window-sill nor the wide scene outside of great stony hills and a valley far below. Neither can he get up and walk around. For he is both blind and legless. As the disease of leprosy advanced, each leg in turn had to be amputated; and blindness also slowly came. Nevertheless he is regarded as the most cheery patient in the Home, the most radiant witness to the transforming power of a Christian experience. Salakwanda Zulu is his name. He dictated his testimony in the Swazi language to Miss Marjory Burne.

The story of Salakwanda's life includes some curious episodes, such as the tale of the occasion when he and some friends smuggled drugs into Johannesburg, outwitting the police by a clever plan. For these and other misdeeds Salakwanda Zulu was at that time quite unrepentant.

> I was not even aware of the fact that I was doing wrong. In my estimation I was a righteous and certainly a clever man. I marvel at my artful ways, for I was not an educated man, but I now realize that I was a tool in the hands of the Devil and full of his wiles.

While he was in Johannesburg Salakwanda fell ill; after a time his disease was diagnosed as leprosy, and so he was compelled to return to Swaziland. But there was no welcome for him at his old home, and he became, like so many more, a wandering outcast. He lived for a time with a group of lepers at a place called Enqabeneni in very bad conditions which aggravated his distress.

> Then one glad day when some Nazarene missionaries came to conduct a service for us I was convicted of my sin through the preaching of the Word. Today I am living at 'Temb'elihle' or 'Good Hope', our new Leprosy Colony at Mbuluzi. God mercifully took me away from Enqabeneni. I am sure I should have died had I remained there. Now, though sightless and without legs, I continually rejoice in the Lord, for I know that He has saved my soul. I am well cared for and have many fine Christian friends, both European and African, some from this country and others from across the seas. I cannot adequately express in words my gratitude to God for all His goodness to me. I love Him supremely. I have the assurance in my heart that when I leave this present world I shall see Jesus face to face— the One who saved me from all my sin. I am waiting for Him to take me to Heaven whenever He chooses to call me. May God be with you all.

He had to wait for a number of years before that call came. In the Spring number of the Mission's magazine for 1960 the testimony from which we have quoted above was reprinted in full, and one sentence is added at the end. 'The prayer of Salakwanda Zulu has been gloriously answered."

In 1958 Mr. Bernard C. Studd, at that time Chairman of the Council of the Mission, went with his wife to renew their acquaintance with India where they had spent many years. They took the opportunity to visit Purulia, Karigiri, Vellore, and Vadathorasalur. Mr. Studd's comment on Purulia is true in a wider context:

> The whole atmosphere of Purulia, as indeed at all other centres, was one of cheerfulness and willingness, everyone working, giving as well as taking. This is a feature of all Mission to Lepers centres, often in marked contrast to secular institutions where too often patients are not

encouraged to work, with the result that they sit about and grumble. The answer lies to a large extent in the difference in motive. In the case of secular institutions the motive is compulsion to safeguard the health of the general public. In a Christian institution the motive is compassion to help sufferers and help them to get back to a normal life.

Mr. and Mrs. Studd then went on to Hay Ling Chau, their visit coinciding with the opening of the Maxwell Memorial Medical Centre. Mr. Studd shared Sunday morning worship with staff and patients in the 'Lord Wills Church'. This was a simple temporary building which the patients had asked for. They said they themselves had houses, and therefore the Lord who was willing to heal them should have His House, too. So they built it as an offering of thanksgiving to Him.

Another tour was undertaken by the Executive Secretary in 1958. He visited 16 stations in India, held four Regional Conferences for superintendents and other senior workers, and brought back to the Council a series of recommendations, most of which were implemented in due course. The most interesting part of this journey was his first visit to Nepal, in the company of Mr. William Bailey, where he engaged in conference with representatives of the United Mission to Nepal on the terms of the proposed co-operation, considered with Dr. Chandy the out-patient work being carried on in part of the large building used by the United Mission, inspected the proposed site of the new leprosy hospital about ten miles out of Kathmandu, and discussed on the spot its possibilities and certain practical problems such as water supply (involving lifting water several hundred feet from a stream at the foot of the site), communications over a bad road, buildings, and lay-out. While at Kathmandu he said he had the unusual experience of calling upon two ambassadors in one day—the Indian and the British—both of whom were encouraging in their attitude and promised their support for the new scheme.

The last visit to the field paid by the Millers took place from October 15th, 1958, to March 10th, 1959. In India this tour covered much the same ground as the previous tour and was then extended to Korea, Hay Ling Chau, and Hong Kong. The main object of the General Secretary was to carry a stage further the new schemes already under consideration for Nepal and Korea and pass in review the state of the work in the various places visited. Special attention was given to Karigiri in South India, where there was a full discussion of the importance of co-operative working with the Christian Medical College, Vellore, the need for a continuing and adequate staff, finance and such matters. The India part of the tour ended at Poladpur. Here the advent of Dr. and Mrs. V. P. Das had opened a new chapter and made it almost 'miraculously different' from what it once was.

Apart from the schemes already described the Mission made a number of grants for work at aided stations—in Africa at Arua in Uganda, at Chissamba in Angola, at Fiwila in Northern Rhodesia, at Lambarene (Dr. Schweitzer's hospital) in Gabon, at Uburu as part of the Ogoja scheme in Nigeria, and for work in the Sudan; in India at Sambalpur, Satara, and Sarengo; in Nepal at Pokhra; in Malaya at Singapore; in Papua at Orokolo, and even a proposed pioneer project in Vietnam. The list could be extended at great length. Then there were the usual routine grants to established stations in India and Burma owned by the Mission, to keep property in good repair, with many special grants for the modernization of old buildings or the provision of new facilities. Most of the latter had been recommended in the reports of secretarial tours, together with some quite large grants to aided work in Africa—new church buildings at Itesio, Kocira and Kumi/Ongino, a new hospital at Itu, new huts at Lambarene, a dispensary at Yoseki, provision for healthy children at Uzuakoli, financial support for Miss Dorothy Lowe at Nyankanda and for Miss Whisson and Miss Samuel at Kuluva—another long list. But most important in this period was the Lucknow Conference of 1953, to which we now turn our attention.

Chapter Ten
IN CONFERENCE

WHEN THE MISSION adopted its new constitution in 1921 provision was made for the formation of an International Committee if the need were to arise. Thirty years later this far-seeing provision was implemented and the Council began to consider a plan for an International Conference of the whole Mission, in co-operation with American Leprosy Missions, at a centre convenient to personnel scattered so widely on the Field and at the Home Bases. This was to be the first Conference of its kind, and, as far as we are aware, the first Missionary Conference ever to be devoted to the subject of leprosy work. Long before the delegates gathered together much thought and prayer had been given to the Conference and its chosen theme, 'Life More Abundant'.

The Council finally decided, in consultation with the Board of American Leprosy Missions, that the Conference should not be held at any one of the home bases but in India, the Mission's largest field of service. This would give delegates from other countries an opportunity to see leprosy work on their way to the Conference or after it had concluded its business. So on Saturday, November 7th, 1953, the Conference assembled in Lucknow, North India.

The outstanding first impression was one of unity in a wide diversity. Donald Miller made this point in his speech at the formal opening session when he described the constitution of the Conference and its representative character.

> This is a Conference of selected delegates, and not a public Congress. For geographical and financial reasons the India delegation is out of proportion to delegations from other lands. But while there is this weightage of India representatives there are delegates from Japan, Siam, Hong Kong, Burma, Pakistan, Uganda, the Union of South Africa, Belgian Congo, Portuguese Cameroons, Nigeria, Greece, Switzerland, Denmark, Great Britain, Ireland, the United States of America, Canada, Australia and New Zealand.

Some are sponsored by the Mission to Lepers; others by the Mission's grown-up daughter across the Atlantic, American Leprosy Missions. Of these delegates many are doctors, including some of the world's leading leprologists; others come from lands happily free of leprosy where Christian folk desire to show their goodwill and faith by exercising the duty and privilege of the strong to help the weak. Some care for children; some engage in caring for the spiritual and social needs of patients; some raise funds; others spend them. But all in this respect are one. They are one in their obedience, however imperfect, to the compassionate Lord Jesus, Who establishes their faith in the equal value before God of every man, Who evokes their own compassion, and Who lifts into one new dimension the ordinarily divided dimensions of time and eternity, physical and spiritual.

His Excellency Sri K. M. Munshi, the Governor of Uttar Pradesh, took the chair, and, though a Hindu, invited the Bishop of Lucknow to open with prayer, thus acknowledging the distinctive Christian character of the Conference. He was supported by Rajkumari Amrit Kaur, Minister for Health, Central Government of India, and the Hon. C. B. Gupta, Minister for Health, Uttar Pradesh Government. The importance of the Conference was thus recognized at the highest levels. Nor was it a mere perfunctory recognition. Rajkumari Amrit Kaur not only had princely blood in her veins ('Rajkumari' might be translated 'Princess'); she was one of the few Christians who attained distinction and cabinet rank in India, and so was able to speak directly to the Conference in the language of a fellow-disciple of the Lord Jesus Christ.

I am glad to note that the general theme for the Conference is 'Life More Abundant'. This means that you will rightly be focusing attention on the economic and social aspects of the work both within institutions and without. It is of the utmost importance that leprosy patients should develop a sense of self-respect. They should not be made to suffer from a feeling of inferiority merely because of the fact that they happen to develop this dread disease. But any psychological change on the part of the patients themselves cannot alone help to rectify matters. What is far more important is that the attitude of the community at large towards the unfortunate victims of the disease should change, and the social ostracism to which they are subjected should disappear altogether.

In conclusion she made an important reference to the attitude of the Government of India to the work of missionaries, and ended a stirring speech with these words:

I am sure they will always be welcome here not only in their personal capacity, not only for the service they render and the example they set, but also as harbingers of international goodwill. I am sure too they will work with us to relieve distress, to banish ignorance, and to build up the India of our dreams. In such work there can be no question of caste or creed or racial barriers, for the human family is indeed one. That is surely the Gospel which the Lord Jesus preached and for which He gave His life a ransom for many.

The Conference received an equally warm welcome from the Christian community in Lucknow. On the first Sunday morning the Conference took part in a Communion Service at Christ Church at which the Rt. Rev. C. J. G. Robinson, Bishop of Lucknow, offered to all the delegates, whatever their Church affiliation might be, the hospitality of the Lord's Table.

We came in our diversity of tradition and practice— Anglican, Presbyterian, Congregationalist, Quaker, Methodist, the Brethren, Baptist, Syrian, Greek Orthodox, and many more—and at that place we were one. It was to all the members of the Conference, and to many friends resident in Lucknow, a striking example of Christian unity at the point where unity is most to be desired, and the lesson of that wonderful service went home to many hearts.

The theme of the Conference was dealt with in a long series of discussions covering all aspects of the work. These discussions were opened by leaders in the various fields of activity in which the Mission is engaged, and were then developed and illustrated by questions or contributions from the floor of the Conference.

At one point the Conference was asked to consider how far Christian compassion should go. A speaker thought that when our Lord said, 'Cleanse the lepers', He did not envisage what we call the leprosy problem. As far as we can tell, this was for Him the problem of the individual sufferer, not the social problem on a large scale, and there is in the New Testament no clear direction as to how far love must go to meet need in the mass. This need is worldwide, or nearly so, and the delegate said it was so great as to be beyond the power of all the Churches combined to meet it, even if they had no other object of their compassion and service.

The Medical Committee of the Conference took a similar view and stated that an effective attack on leprosy would need the co-ordinated planning and effort of central government, local government, and voluntary agencies, such planning being still absent in many countries. Here is a part of the judgement of the Medical Committee:

> It would therefore call the attention of the authorities to the need in each endemic area of an appropriate representative body to plan, develop, and co-ordinate the work. It is emphasized that government should be represented on this body at the highest level, so that accepted recommendations will be followed by effective action. Only when government, missions, and other voluntary organizations, the community and the leprosy patients themselves, recognize each their own responsibility, will the result be commensurate with the energy spent. Failure of such recognition by any one of these groups will hamper the efforts of the others and cause delay in the control of the disease.

Even so, it was recognized that there is such a thing as a specific Christian contribution to leprosy work, a quality of service which can be rendered just because those who give it are followers of the Lord Jesus Christ.

Dr. R. G. Cochrane contended that:

> While it is not the business of Christian missions to meet the need in the mass, as we have called it, it *is* our business to show how need can be met in this Christian spirit.

Accept the limited range of compassion, and concentrate every resource and the whole weight of the Christian witness within the selected area of service.

This is a sample of the kind of discussion which arose on certain broad issues, and it is a sample selected not because the opinions of 20 years ago are to be accepted as infallible, but because the basic question is still with us. How far should Christian compassion go? Is there any limit to the outreach of a Spreading Tree like The Leprosy Mission? If so, where is that limit, and what conditions will impose it?

For the rest, there were displays of various kinds, mostly in the evenings—literature, visual aid materials, slides and films including one fascinating film of Paul Brand operating on 'claw hand'.

The final day, Monday November 16th was by no means least in interest and importance, for the whole Conference went out to Faizabad, 80 miles away, for the official opening of the Wellesley Bailey Children's Sanatorium, so appropriately built at this place where the founder of the Mission decided to give up his career in the Indian Police and become a missionary. In the popular version of the Conference report this memorable event is described:

> It was a brilliant scene, full of colour, light and movement, and a fitting illustration of the way life more abundant can flow out to accomplish the Lord's will. It was a joyous occasion too, the laughter of the children mingling in our memory with the skirl of the bagpipes of the Police Band and the applause which greeted Dr. Chandy in acknowledgement of his part and witness during the last 15 years. Donald Miller was a happy man that day as he recalled the first time he saw the Faizabad site, and now looked upon the desert that had already blossomed as the rose, and soon would bring forth fairer flowers and richer harvests. Raymond Currier, who as Executive Secretary of American Leprosy Missions had been asked to perform the opening ceremony, said how deeply he appreciated this honour, and these were not conventional words uttered by polite lips. There was for him and for all who took part, down to the smallest of the children, a joyous sense

of thanksgiving for God's goodness. We were all honoured, we were all blessed; for we were privileged to see a striking example of Christian love in action, as the ministering hand, moved by the compassionate heart and informed by the understanding mind, reached out across the world to heal and save.

It was evident that the leprosy cause engaged the skills of many very able people; this had never before been so clearly demonstrated for the very good reason that never before had they been brought together in this way.

Here is surely the reason why the Conference in Lucknow was so important. We all knew that the Mission was international as well as interdenominational, but for most of us this knowledge was theoretical and somewhat vague. Now for the first time in the 89 years of the Mission's history all parts of the Spreading Tree came together in a living reality —representatives of the Council in London and the Board in New York, delegates from all the Auxiliaries, technical experts, workers on the field, doctors, nurses, educationists, administrators, pastors, 'All together in one place'.

The effect was more than stimulating; it was uplifting, even inspiring, for surely there was an outpouring of the Spirit in those Lucknow days. All concerned learned a great deal from one another and this knowledge took on new dimensions. The parochial view was forgotten as wider horizons opened out. There came to every delegate a new vision of the greatness of this ministry in which we were called to serve. There was a deeper sense of committal and rededication in obedience to the Lord's command, and after Lucknow the Auxiliaries began to respond more and more to the challenge of need and the call to personal service.

We should mention here another area in which the Mission made an advance—the International Leprosy Congress or, as it was later called, the International Congress of Leprology, a significant change of title indicating in itself progress in the scientific study of the disease. For many years a Vice-President of the Mission, Dr. Ernest Muir, had taken a leading part in successive Congresses and the Mission was otherwise represented in Havana, Cuba, in April 1948, at Madrid in 1953, just prior to the Mission's Conference in Lucknow, and again in Tokyo in November 1958. There is a steady progression in the increasing strength of the Mission's delegations to these Congresses. Donald Miller's tour in 1958 and 1959 included attendance at this Congress at Tokyo, and in his report he mentions the prominence of the Mission delegation in the work of the special panels of the Congress, particularly that on orthopaedic surgery. He himself was a member of the Social Aspects Committee and drafted its report. Paul Brand's film *Lifted Hands* was shown at the Congress and made a profound impression. The Congress, said Donald Miller, was notable for its humanity, its unity of spirit, based on a more widely shared knowledge, and its 'atmosphere of reasonable hope'.

The reader may have noticed that earlier in this chapter the American Society has been referred to under a new name. In 1949 New York informed London that at their next Annual General Meeting the name of the Mission in America was to be changed to American Leprosy Missions Incorporated. No action was called for on the part of the London Council as the American Society had full autonomy. The Council merely recorded the change with a message of goodwill to New York, and the only immediate result as far as this Mission was concerned was another rather inconclusive discussion about the use of the word 'Lepers' in the Mission's own title. The time had not yet come for serious consideration of such a change, nor could the Mission at this stage change the title of the magazine, *Without the Camp*. After consultation with the Auxiliaries overseas it was evident that there was no unanimity of opinion and this idea also was dropped for the time being, to be taken up again much later.

In the national Auxiliaries there were naturally a number of changes in personnel between the end of World War II and 1960. Mr. Robert Edgar was appointed Secretary of the Australian Auxiliary in 1946. The Rev. H. W. Konkle resigned the Secretaryship of Canada in 1947, and in the same year Dr. T. B. M. Sloan succeeded Dr. Turner as Secretary for

Scotland. Mr. Wynne also retired that year and Mr. R. B. McCandless took his place as Secretary of the North of Ireland District. In 1948 the Rev. Walter B. Elliott was relieved of the main burden of his work, though he continued for some years to give assistance as an Associate Secretary, and the Rev. Brian L. Gandon succeeded him as Secretary for England and Wales, while the Rev. G. Howard King, B.A., B.D., was appointed Secretary for Canada. Another important appointment about this time was that of the Rev. Murray H. Feist, B.A., who brought new vigour to the New Zealand Auxiliary so that it rapidly increased its income. Mr. Gandon gave five years of service to England and Wales, and in 1953 the Rev. W. Hedley Ennals entered on this important work and carried its burden till the end of 1958. Mr. G. Newberry Fox, who had been a member of Council since 1944, then made a generous offer of service which was gratefully accepted by the Council and withdrew from his business commitments to take over the England and Wales Auxiliary. In the meantime the Rev. Charles Ellis had resigned and the Rev. C. C. du Heaume became Secretary for Ireland in 1956.

During the period we are now considering the Spreading Tree put out three more of its 'aerial roots'. One of these resulted in the establishment of the Hong Kong Auxiliary, which has already been noted; the other two were Denmark and Southern Africa. In each case the first steps were taken in 1946. The Rev. Frank Oldrieve, formerly the Mission's Secretary for India, and later working with the British Empire Leprosy Relief Association, had made an approach to the Mission with a view to organizing an Auxiliary in the Union of South Africa and the Rhodesias, and in 1947 he was appointed Secretary for a period of two years. Unfortunately he died suddenly after only about nine months, while the interim Committee for Southern Africa was still in process of formation. The Rev. R. S. W. Ford was appointed in his place, and by 1950 the constitution of the new Auxiliary had been formally approved and its first meeting had been held with the Archbishop of Cape Town as President.

In his report to the Council, following a visit in 1950, the

General Secretary said that the atmosphere in this part of Africa was very different from that of Australia and New Zealand. He and his wife had travelled about 3000 miles in South Africa, had addressed many meetings, and had visited three leprosy institutions. There appeared to be an opportunity for the Mission to act as a 'bridge' in bringing together diverse elements in a common cause. It was also realized that the Southern Africa Auxiliary would have to determine its own lines of approach to the public, especially with reference to leprosy work in Africa. Mr. Ford and the members of his Committee skilfully found the way to further the cause of the Mission in subsequent and even more difficult years.

The establishment of the Danish Auxiliary was a simpler matter. Many friends in Denmark were already interested in the work of Miss Lillelund at Vadathorasalur and in the Danish Mission work at Sikonge in Tanganyika. When Donald Miller went to Copenhagen in September 1947 he was received with 'much cordiality' and a working committee was established forthwith. The very next month, on October 15th of the same year, the Denmark Auxiliary held its first meeting with the Bishop of Copenhagen as President and Miss Anna Wiesel as Secretary and Treasurer.

Events in the other overseas Auxiliaries were of a more routine nature. In 1950 preparations were made for the formation of the Mission to Lepers (New Zealand) Auxiliary with a constitution similar to that of Australia, but adapted to New Zealand needs, and this constitution was formally approved by the Council in 1955. There were also revisions of the constitutions of the Auxiliaries in Scotland and Ireland. After the Lucknow Conference of 1953 these Auxiliaries began to take a more prominent part in the shaping of policy. In 1959, for instance, the Secretary for New Zealand, the Rev. Murray H. Feist, visited London and met a special Committee to discuss certain proposals made by his Council relating to representation of New Zealand on the Council of the Mission, closer relations between the Auxiliaries and the Council, and the possibility of the allocation of fields of special interest which might become a first charge on funds raised in New

Zealand. One outcome of this discussion was the suggestion that the International Committee of the Mission should meet at regular intervals of about five years. This proposal was taken up and resulted in a meeting of the United Consultative Committee, as it came to be called, in 1962.

How had it become possible for the Mission to embark on so many projects which must have involved considerable expenditure? The answer is found in a remarkable rise in the Mission's income. Just four figures taken at five-year intervals show clearly the upward trend. In each year at the March meeting of the Council the financial position up to the end of the previous year was reported, subject to audit, with the following result: -

Total ordinary income	1945	…	…	£103,403
,, ,, ,,	1950	…	…	£133,353
,, ,, ,,	1955	…	…	£226,962
,, ,, ,,	1960	…	…	£441,558

Similarly, there was an increase in the income derived from legacies as more and more friends remembered the Mission in their wills. In 1945 legacies amounted to nearly £15,000, in 1950 £30,000, in 1955 £41,000 and in 1961 (the figure for 1960 is not given in the Minutes of the Council) £50,600.

The Mission was in fact able to build up reserves which enabled the Council to make a most generous gesture in 1954 as part of the celebration of the Eightieth Anniversary of the founding of the Mission. This was to offer the sum of £80,000—£1,000 for each year of the Mission's existence—to co-operating Societies in Great Britain and Ireland to enable them to erect or improve buildings, or provide equipment or transport for approved schemes for leprosy work. 37 Societies were invited to make suggestions and most of them did so. The sum of £66,700 was distributed in this way, and the balance of this Birthday Fund was later used for the Mission's own projects.

At Headquarters, in addition to the appointment of an Executive Secretary (the Rev. Wilfrid H. Russell) the staff was further strengthened. The Rev. Harold T. Barrow was appointed Secretary for Youth Work with effect from the beginning of 1947. He inaugurated the 'Order of Lamplighters' to enlist the interest of children and this movement had success in Great Britain and Eire. There were also encouraging reports from other countries, especially New Zealand, but after some years the original impetus appears to have been lost, and the problem of bringing in the support of young people remained, though there was from time to time evidence that the Mission's work did have an appeal for youth. Miss Joyce Reason joined the Headquarters staff as Editorial Secretary on September 1st 1951 for a five-year term of valuable service. She is remembered for her book *Laughter in the Desert* which she wrote after her visit to stations in Uganda and Tanganyika in 1952. The Rev. Walter Fancutt succeeded her as Editorial Secretary in May 1957. His literary flair showed itself in the style and content of the Mission's magazine and, most notably, in the Prayer Guide which he produced. Another appointment was very welcome. Dr. Neil D. Fraser had been having increasing trouble with an arthritic hip and in due course had a successful operation while on furlough in England. This gave him much relief, but he did not return to Hong Kong. By this time his work at Hay Ling Chau was well established and could be left in other capable hands, and he was appointed Medical Secretary early in 1960. He proved to be a valuable addition to Headquarters staff. His wide experience of leprosy work and his down-to-earth approach to its practical problems were a great help in the years that followed. There was one notable loss when Mr. William Hayward died on September 19th, 1956. His remarkable record of service has already been mentioned in Chapter 7.

With the passing of the years there were also inevitable changes in the Officers of the Mission and in the membership of the Council. Mr. A. T. Barber, one of the few remaining links with the founder of the Mission, died in 1949 in his eighty-fifth year, and Sir Walter S. Kinnear, K.B.E., Chairman of the Council, in 1953. He was a distinguished Civil Servant and brought to the Chairmanship special qualities of mind and heart, as Donald Miller reminds us:

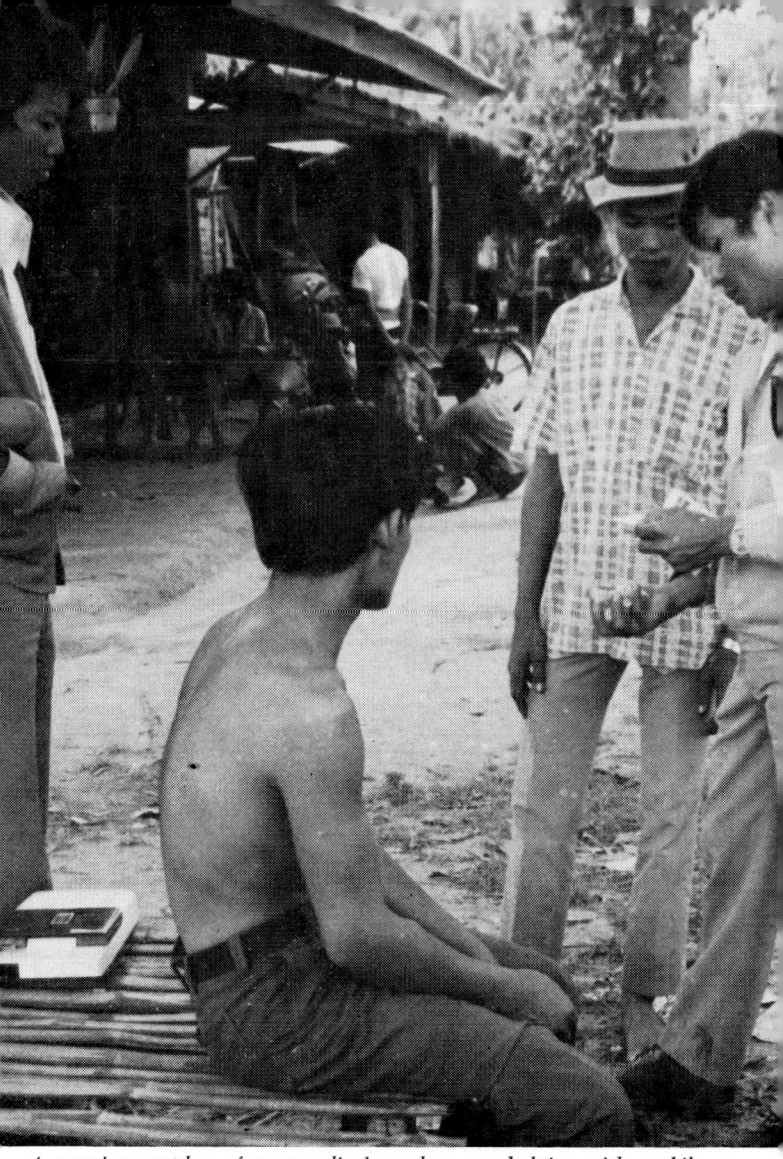

A growing number of paramedical workers are helping with mobile clinics, education programmes, and rural surveys. Here, at Manorom, Thailand, a young worker explains needed treatment to a patient's friend, while the cassette player conveys the Good News.

Occupational therapy is good for hands and for morale. Here, at Purulia, Mrs. M. Simms, the wife of the Mission's President, watches busy fingers recovering vital skills.

It was God's good gift to the Mission that at the time when a new Chairman of Council was required upon the death in 1943 of Mr. Walter B. Sloan, Sir Walter Kinnear's years of public service had come to a close and he was free to accept the invitation made to him. He had been a member of the Council from its inauguration in London in 1921, and was familiar with the work. As a Christian Irishman he made an invaluable link in London with the land in which the Mission was born. Now, in the middle years of the War, he became the Council's leader, and very soon the impress of his personality was felt. A large heart was matched with a large mind. Sir Walter quickly searched for and found the central core of any situation or problem; and then he kept it central, thereby allowing all other subsidiary issues to fall into their proper place. In consequence broad policies, whether in the organization of support or in the prosecution of the Mission's primary tasks, emerged clear and uncomplicated. And during the years that followed, our Chairman, leading an increasingly enthusiastic and devoted company of counsellors, played a notable part in moulding all the developments which have since taken place.

In 1959 the Council received with regret the resignation of the President of the Mission, the Most Rev. J. A. Fitzgerald Gregg, D.D., following his retirement as Primate of All Ireland. Later in the year His Grace the Archbishop of Canterbury (Dr. Fisher) accepted the invitation to become the President of the Mission.

Sir Maurice Hallett followed Mr. Dallimore as Honorary Treasurer in 1953, and in the same year Mr. Bernard C. Studd was elected Chairman of the Council in succession to Sir Walter Kinnear.

In 1958 Donald Miller reminded the Chairman of the Council that he would reach the normal age for retirement in August of that year. Just before his actual retirement the Council had the pleasure of congratulating Mr. Miller on the award of the M.B.E. to him in the New Year's Honours List of 1960. Later in that year he withdrew from the room at No. 7 Bloomsbury Square which he had entered for the first time as General Secretary on that January day in 1943. No doubt he did so with mixed feelings. But there was no question at all about the tribute paid to him in the magazine article written by Mr. Studd. He gave an outline of Mr. Miller's career, so full of variety and incident, spoke of the versatility shown in his books and pictures, and ended the article with a reference to the deeper qualities which he saw:

> He combined a sympathy and compassion for the suffering with dedicated obedience to his Lord and Saviour. Showing in everything great love, great understanding and wise statesmanship, he was Christ-like in thought, Christ-like in outlook, and Christ-like in action.

Earlier in the article Mr. Studd had made a remark which must not be overlooked:

> That he should have been able to give so many years of full service is little short of miraculous, for he emerged from the 1914-18 War with his health seriously impaired and a medical verdict, 'Go easy for the rest of your life'. So said the doctors, but once again the Old Testament promise was to be proved true. 'As thy days so shall thy strength be'. What an amazing full life the next forty years were to produce!

A wonderful record indeed, as Mr. Studd says, for which the whole Mission continues to give thanks.

Part Four

**WIDER AND WIDER YET
(1960 - 1970)**

Chapter Eleven
FIVE FRUITFUL YEARS

WHEN THE REV. Wilfrid H. Russell was nominated to be the Mission's General Secretary it was decided at his suggestion that he be appointed 'for a period of four years with the possibility of extension by one year'. To maintain continuity in central administration it was desirable that the General Secretary should hold office for at least ten years, and preferably for a longer period, as Messrs Anderson and Miller had done. But this was now not possible, because Miller and Russell were too near to one another in age. It therefore seemed advisable to establish an administration to take charge for a limited period while the Council looked for a General Secretary who was young enough to expect to serve for ten years or so. As it turned out the new General Secretary did continue in office for that fifth year—*i.e.,* until 1965. This chapter therefore covers the period 1960 to 1965, the five years of his administration.

The new General Secretary regarded himself as the first among equals, and whatever 'leadership' would be required would be the leadership of a team. He therefore immediately instituted at Headquarters a weekly meeting of Secretaries, designed to give his colleagues an opportunity to discuss together and with him the work on which they were engaged at the time, and to ensure that all this was co-ordinated and directed along the main lines of policy laid down by the Council. This weekly Secretaries' meeting was a success, and in due time Mr. Russell's successor carried on the same tradition of regular harmonious consultation and co-operative effort. Moreover, the same principle came to be applied more widely. As we shall see later, the meeting of the United Consultative Committee of 1962 was designed to encourage the same team spirit by drawing the national Auxiliaries more and more from the circumference to a central unity of concerted action.

Wilfrid Russell was given strong support by the two Chairmen of Council under whom he had the honour to serve—Mr. Bernard Studd and Sir Harry Greenfield—and indeed by the whole Council. Moreover, he had a fine team to work with. Donald Miller had indeed retired as General Secretary, but he was retained as Consultant to be called upon when his advice was required. Dr. N. D. Fraser served most acceptably as Medical Secretary and also took over responsibility for candidates for missionary service and for general oversight of the Africa field, leaving the General Secretary free to concentrate on the work east of Suez. The Rev. Walter Fancutt had charge of the Mission magazine and other publications, and of visual-aid material of several kinds, including films and film-strips. Mr. F. G. Torrie Attwell, who had previously been the Accounts Secretary, was now appointed Financial Secretary, a tribute both to his personal ability and to the growing importance of his small but efficient department. Finally, Mr. G. Newberry Fox, as Secretary for England and Wales, completed the team.

Short though this period of five years was, there was nothing static about it. There were, for instance, a number of visits overseas. The General Secretary went East in 1961 and again in 1963; the Medical Secretary visited Africa in 1961 and went even further afield the next year, to New Zealand and Australia, Papua/New Guinea, Korea and Hong Kong, and again to Africa in 1963; the Editorial Secretary visited India and Nepal in 1962, and in 1964 the Financial Secretary was able to see some of the India centres which for years had been only names to him.

The travels of the General Secretary provide a convenient framework for noting the many and varied developments of the Mission's activities, but this necessarily restricts the viewpoint to that of the London Headquarters—a limitation which we acknowledge, with apologies to those in the Auxiliaries who may well feel that there were other viewpoints which have been neglected.

The tenth anniversary of the establishment of the Hong Kong Auxiliary was celebrated in 1961. The Marianne Reichl Aid to Lepers Group, a company of ladies resident in Hong

Kong had given remarkable support to the work of the Mission, and Mr. Russell was glad to meet them. The Christmas Fair, held less than a month before his visit, produced about 85,000 Hong Kong dollars, more than £5,000 sterling.

On the Isle of Happy Healing he found further evidence of the strength of the support given by the Hong Kong community in the recent erection of a new workshop and of cottages for children, with plans for a school, the cost to be met by the Hong Kong Auxiliary. There was also some discussion of a scheme for a new church building.

The opening of the work on the island Hay Ling Chau corresponded roughly with the tenth birthday of the Hong Kong Auxiliary. What had been achieved there during the past decade? Beryl Batstone gave the answer in an article in the magazine of 1962:

> The best way to assess the result of the strenuous endeavours of the last ten years or so is to come and see! Very many individuals, groups, medical visitors, students, church parties and missionaries do just that. Let us join them and step aboard the Mission's sturdy but swift motor vessel, the *Ling Hong*, and settle down in a deck-chair to enjoy the breeze and the blueness of sea and sky, as the harbour recedes and the shadowy outlines on the horizon emerge as scattered islands and rocks. Before long one island becomes the centre of interest as the *Ling Hong* steadily sails towards it, and you become aware of its greater greenness, thick pine woods, and sparkling beaches. Soon you are stepping on to a wide stone pier and walking towards the shade of the large Flame of the Forest trees on the jetty, while a Chinese or Western member of the staff makes you feel welcome.
>
> Before the afternoon is over you will have seen the patients' attractive stone cottage homes and workshops, and walked through the main valley with its fields and terraces, busy agricultural areas, and careful irrigation and composting systems. All around are busy and active people intent on their duties as farmers or gardeners, pig, duck, and rabbit keepers. Others are working as masons, painters, carpenters, bamboo workers, fitters, plumbers, bean-curd makers, cobblers, or electricians busy in the humming

generator house. Wood carvers, marquetry and model makers, rattan workers, anti-malarial squad, barbers, storekeepers, boatmen, librarians, laundry workers and cooks are all actively at work!

Sorrow is there too, walking the paths hand-in-hand with adult and child alike for, as a senior staff member recently said, it would be quite wrong to imagine that our patients exist in a state of care-free bliss. They have deep and distressing problems, but still the amazing fact is that the prevailing atmosphere is one of such hope and confidence.

Miss Batstone ends her article with a reference to the sustained life and activity of the Church fellowship which was present on the island and had, she says, been there since the first day.

The Church is interdenominational, but is closely linked with the Chinese Lutheran Church who supply the pastor and have taken patients into their Bible School for training as lay preachers and evangelists. Last year there were 123 men and 49 women communicant Church members, and regular enquirers and catechism classes are held. There are the usual meetings for prayer and Bible study, Sunday School and Youth Groups, choir practices, deacons' meetings, women's meetings and social activities. Some patients respond quickly and eagerly to the Gospel message, but many others have no sense of personal need. Perhaps the most effective form of evangelism is the example of a nucleus of really keen Christian patients, who can testify gladly and effectively to the saving power of Christ in their own lives, and from a shared background of disease and sorrow. Under the faithful leadership of the Pastor, the Church is a growing one, conscious of spiritual responsibility and meeting the challenge. As with all Christian endeavour there is opposition and heart-break from time to time. This is especially true when church members are discharged and are afraid to transfer their membership in case their connection with a leprosarium comes to light. When this happens real trouble can arise resulting in the unhappy believer leaving, and being unwilling to expose himself to further ostracism and disgrace. Follow-up work is made difficult because of this fear, but some do find a

Church home and fellowship after their discharge, and we believe that time and prayer is lessening the difficulties and sorrows too frequently experienced now.

Miss Batstone ends on a note of thanksgiving.

It is thrilling to see men and women, girls and boys, made whole. Not only are they receiving new life and healing spiritually, as in all the past years of the Mission's worldwide ministry, but now they can receive physical healing as well. Nowhere is this combined onslaught against sickness and sorrow more rewarding than on this small island. The staff and patients join in praising God for all His grace and healing power so richly manifested to them in the past ten years.

From Hong Kong the General Secretary went on to Korea where the weather gave him a cold reception.

One main object of the visit to Korea was to see the site, three miles outside Taegu, which had been purchased for the building of the proposed Mission centre. The site was a sloping one with a rather narrow frontage, but the American-trained architect, Mr. Zaiong Zo, had excellent ideas (and an American bulldozer) for making terraces on which the necessary buildings could be erected. As soon as the winter frost had loosened its grip on the ground, the work went ahead so well that by the end of the year the General Secretary was able to write about the 'Korean Prospect':

One of the buildings is already complete. This will be the administration block, and contains accommodation for a garage, a generating set for electricity supply, and an office and store. Other buildings in course of erection are quarters for Korean staff and, at the top of the hill, the house which Mr. and Mrs. Lloyd will occupy, sharing it with Dr. Wilson, and another house for Miss Butterworth and Miss Grace Bennett. The plan is taking form and substance. But perhaps the greatest change is in the outlook, the Korean prospect. In place of the bleak, bare cold of January there is now a vista of paddy fields flooded with water for the early summer planting. Before these words appear in print they will have turned first to a vivid green and then to a dull gold. Winter is far behind, and the earth exultantly speaks of harvest. Yes, harvest! Already there begins to appear in the Korean prospect the promise of those harvest fields to which the Lord Jesus called us to lift up our eyes. Thankfully we obey, and gladly we lift up our hearts also in hope and faith and in prayer for this new enterprise.

In discussions with Dr. Lee, the Dean of the Medical School at Taegu, and Dr. Suh, Superintendent of the Medical College Hospital, Messrs. Russell and Lloyd heard of a scheme for the development of the Government hospital at Taegu which might include a leprosy section provided by the Mission on terms to be agreed. This in fact came to be; it was an important step forward because the Medical College Hospital at Taegu not only had the prestige of an institution supported by the Korean Government, but was also a strategic centre for an anti-leprosy campaign, as it was a teaching hospital where medical students could be given the right ideas about leprosy and its treatment. The influence of a Mission leprosy unit established at such a centre could therefore spread far and wide. This plan, like that for the Mission centre, also went forward without delay. Money was made available for the building and its equipment—nearly £25,000 in all—and in December 1962 the Rev. James Waddell, the Mission's Secretary for the Far East, went over to Korea at Mr. Lloyd's invitation to be present at the formal opening of the new Medical Centre on the afternoon of Saturday, 1st December. Mr. Waddell commented:

High appreciation was expressed of the Mission to Lepers' initial contribution to leprosy work in Korea some 50 years before, and of the new lead given during these past four years culminating in the erection of this new leprosy centre in the University Medical College grounds. The three-storey building has its own gateway and porch entrance to an outpatient department on the ground floor; wards for 20 inpatients, a well-equipped operating theatre and a physiotherapy unit on the first floor; and staff rooms and administration office on the top floor. The design is attractive, the construction excellent, and the whole reflects great credit on the architect and all who contributed to the planning and equipping.

At its December meeting in 1962 the Council had the pleasure of congratulating the Rev. C. M. Lloyd and his colleagues on the award to him of the Public Service Medal by the President of the Republic of Korea. All rejoiced that the Mission's workers, and especially the leader of the Mission team in Korea, came to be honoured in this particular way, but it was Mrs. Lloyd who told a story to illustrate the fact that in the Korean enterprise, and indeed in the Mission's work everywhere, 'we are all involved', to use her own words.

We have had a very hot summer in Korea this year, and Taegu, the town where we live, has the reputation of being the coldest spot in the country in winter and the hottest in summer! It was on a very hot day, with a temperature around 98 degrees, that at five o'clock one evening we found a young man sitting on our doorstep. With badly ulcerated feet, emaciated and completely exhausted with the heat and walking, he had sunk down on the doorstep of the Mission to Lepers' house where, he had been told, he would receive help.

We admitted him for a period of rest and treatment. Later, it was necessary for us to find a permanent shelter for him, and this we were able to do at Andong, a leprosy colony seventy miles out of Taegu, where the Mission makes a grant-in-aid. On the appointed day we got our patient into the Landrover and duly arrived at Andong. There the difficulty of getting him out of the car was immediately solved by one of the many patients who quickly gathered round offering his back, so that he could be taken pick-a-back to the treatment room. The last we saw of him was when he was being given another pick-a-back down the road to the accommodation provided for him in the men's section, the bundle of bedding and clothes we had provided being carried by another patient. The comforting and sheltering of this poor man was accomplished, though not designedly, by a sequence of kindly and co-operative acts. First of all, there were those who told him to go to the Mission to Lepers' centre in Taegu. Then, on arriving at the Medical College Hospital in Taegu, on which compound we were living, there was the gatekeeper who admitted him and directed him to our house; there was the doctor who decided that here was a man who must receive help and succour at once, even though he could not be permanently housed in our unit; there was the Korean nurse who, on receiving him into the ward where he was found to have a high temperature, set about removing his dirty and very smelly clothes, giving him a sorely needed bath (this is worthy of special note, as it is not the generally accepted service for Korean nurses to render); there was the Director of the Andong colony who agreed to receive him; there were the men who welcomed him on arrival there as a fellow-sufferer, showing in the most practical way their desire to help by offering their backs to carry him though he was a complete stranger. If we may trace the story further back still, this sequence of co-operation, of course, really started in the hearts and minds of *you* who will read this; who by your gifts and faithful efforts have made it possible for the Mission to be in Korea; have made possible the creation and maintenance of the unit where he was nursed; have supplied the Landrover which transported him seventy miles to Andong; and have donated the bedding and clothing with which he had to be provided.

It is our hope that this experience of co-operative and loving service on the part of so many will help this patient to believe the truth of the Gospel, which he heard preached while he was in our unit and which he will continue to hear at Andong, for there is quite a strong Church in the colony.

On the way home from Korea Wilfrid Russell spent a few days in Burma and saw the Mission's work at Moulmein and Mandalay. At the former, excellent building work had been done by the patients under the leadership of Miss Marion Shivers, the honorary superintendent, and Dr. Edwards. Miss Shivers had raised considerable sums locally, her latest project being the building of a new house for the superintendent at an estimated cost of £2,250, of which £750 had already been collected in Moulmein, the Mission granting the remainder. In Mandalay the co-operation between the local Methodist

Church and the Home was very good, and the medical work ably directed by Dr. Jamal Din. The physiotherapy department under Mr. Kenneth Kin Thein was described in the General Secretary's report as 'at present second only to Karigiri', and the hospital wards were in first-class order under Mrs. Kin Thein, formerly Miss Ruth Thomas, S.R.N., M.C.S.P. Miss Florence Cleaver, the honorary superintendent, put forward a long list of projects, two of which were recommended for grants during the year, and the remainder covered by a five-year plan for reconstruction and development.

A visit to the Indian Homes followed a little more than two years later at the end of 1963, and included three special celebrations—that of the Diamond Jubilee of the Home at Chevayur, Calicut; the seventy-fifth anniversary of the founding of the Purulia Home; and the Silver Jubilee at Faizabad. After meeting a number of distinguished workers at the Christian Medical College, Vellore, Mr. Russell noted that in a place like this 'there is no such thing as a leprologist pure and simple; what I found was a team of highly skilled workers each making his or her contribution to our total knowledge of leprosy'.

A new hospital was opened ten miles from Kathmandu on that beautiful pine-clad hillside which had been named Anandaban, the Forest of Joy (see Isaiah xliv, 23). Some difficult problems had been solved, notably that of the transport of materials to the site over a shockingly bad road and the problem of lifting water several hundred feet from a stream at the foot of the hillside to the site chosen for the main buildings. By the time the General Secretary arrived all was in readiness for the great day, Saturday, November 23rd, 1963; Dr. Chandy and his colleagues were greatly encouraged because His Majesty King Mahendra had promised to come and declare the hospital open.

Then several thousand miles away an event occurred which cast a long shadow across the world—certainly as far as Kathmandu in remote Nepal.

Early in the morning of this long-awaited day the radio brought the shocking news of the assassination of the President of the United States (President Kennedy). At first consternation reigned, as it was realized that the King of Nepal might cancel the function. An urgent message to Kathmandu brought reassuring news later in the morning, and preparations for the event proceeded briskly. By about 11.30 the approach to the hospital was gay with decorations, and seating had been arranged on the dais for the Royal Party and for the numerous guests who were expected to attend the ceremony. Later in the morning, however, Dr. Fleming brought the news that the King had issued a decree for the observance of a day of mourning, and the Royal Party would therefore not attend the function at Anandaban, but the King had graciously suggested that the opening ceremony should proceed without him.

So the ceremony went ahead in the presence of a considerable company in spite of the absence of the Royal Party. After a moment of silence observed as a tribute to President Kennedy's memory, an opening prayer and several speeches, Wilfrid Russell invited the company to inspect the new building. After this tour of inspection tea was served on the flat roof of the lower section, and it proved to be a very fine tea-room with magnificent scenery on all sides, glowing in the brilliant sunshine. The next day, Sunday, was a day given over to thanksgiving, particularly in the afternoon.

Many friends came from Kathmandu to join the staff and the patients and we were a considerable company when we gathered together on the roof of the lower block of the hospital. The setting was very beautiful; all around us the watching hills and, near at hand, the whispering pines, with bright sunshine flooding the whole scene. On this occasion of praise to God Anandaban became in very truth the Forest of Joy. Mr. Jonathan Lindell, Executive Secretary of the United Mission to Nepal, was in charge and he delegated the Act of Thanksgiving to Pastor George who spoke in fluent Nepali. Then Mr. Russell followed with an address based on the text Mr. Oliver had given in his message of greeting—'This is the Lord's doing; it is marvellous in our eyes' (Psalm cxviii, 23). The third part of the service was an act of dedication led by Mr. Lindell in Nepali. Several hymns well sung were interspersed; it was a real service of thanksgiving and gratitude to God. The patients then left us, as there are as yet no baptized believers, and we gathered at the Lord's Table in a simple celebration of Holy Communion. We had no prayer book and repeated from memory the introductory Collect and the Words of Institution. The very simplicity of this service seemed to heighten its effect and, in such a setting, with the loveliness of the valley all around us, we worshipped in the beauty of holiness and with a deep sense of peace. There were 54 communicants and it all seemed to be the perfect end to this day of Thanksgiving.

His Majesty King Mahendra later kept his promise. On April 1st, 1964, in the presence of the Ambassadors of Great Britain, America, and India, and several hundred people, the King of Nepal, his Queen and his Prime Minister, with important Government ministers and officers, visited Anandaban. Dr. P. J. Chandy greeted their Majesties and the guests and led the way to the main gate of the hospital, where Dr. V. P. Das handed a pair of scissors to His Majesty so that he might cut a ribbon tied across the gate.

Before leaving Anandaban the King and Queen showed great pleasure at all they had seen and heard and expressed the hope that the work being done by the Mission would continue to bring success. The Nepali newspapers published lengthy accounts of the royal visit and it is clear that the name Anandaban is fixed in the minds and hearts of a great number of people in Nepal.

While at Purulia the General Secretary had the pleasure of inviting Mr. A. D. Askew, at that time the Superintendent of the Home, to join the staff at Headquarters. Thus it came about that Mr. Askew was formally appointed Executive Secretary, to the great advantage of the work, with effect from 1st July 1965.

The reader may have wondered why Dr. V. P. Das was present at the time of the royal visit to Anandaban, and in what capacity. In order to explain this point we must go back a few years. Mr. William Bailey, M.A., gave many years of service to the Mission after becoming Secretary for India in 1947. Ten years later the Council accepted his suggestion that in some quarters a person calling himself Secretary for India would not be particularly welcome for political reasons (in Pakistan, for instance) and for this reason his designation was changed to that of Secretary for Southern Asia. In view of his increasing responsibilities with the general expansion of the work he was later given Associate Secretaries to assist him in the four main sections of the India field; one of these Associate Secretaries was Dr. V. P. Das, at that time in charge at Poladpur. Dr. Das's ability as a leader of the work was already evident, and in 1960 he was appointed Acting Secretary for Southern Asia during Mr. Bailey's furlough in that year. In 1961 Mr. Bailey resigned from the service of the Mission. Dr. Victor P. Das was appointed to be Secretary for Southern Asia, and it was in this capacity that he took part in the official opening of the new hospital at Kathmandu.

Dr. Neil Fraser made two visits to Africa—to him an entirely new field of leprosy work—the first being in 1961 and the second in 1963. During the first of these he saw about a dozen centres of work, made suggestions for a number of grants for various projects, and gave valuable advice at several stations, particularly with regard to proposed new work at Fiwale Hill in Northern Rhodesia and at Makutupora in Tanganyika. Here he considered with Dr. Hannah and Bishop Stanway some of the questions which would arise when the move was made to the new institution at Hombolo. This project now went forward under the able direction of Mr. W. G. L. Hart, an experienced missionary of the Australian Church Missionary Society, and designated manager of the new institution. His support was undertaken by the New Zealand Auxiliary.

In July and August 1963 Dr. Fraser was able to see at Hombolo the buildings erected under Mr. Hart's supervision;

he settled the details of the transfer of 98 patients from Makutupora, a dozen at a time, and advised regarding their medical treatment and general welfare. The new Home was formally opened by the Hon. Job Lucinde, the Minister of Home Affairs in the Tanganyika Government, on the 25th September 1963, several weeks after Dr. Fraser's visit. The new institution was given the name of 'The Living Water Leprosy Centre', the reference being to the reservoir near by which had in fact led to the choice of this particular site. Dr. Fraser commented:

> A suitable symbol for the Centre would be a Baobab tree with a hospital on one side and a church on the other, all on the bank of a reservoir. The Baobab tree is a typical feature of the Central Tanganyika landscape; its huge trunk stores large quantities of water and, being of no value for fuel, is left standing when other trees are felled. Just as rain makes all sorts of growth and development possible, so the inner springs are there for all who seek them.

Dr. Fraser went on to propose that Hombolo be developed as a Leprosy Centre with facilities for the investigation and treatment of patients, the training of crippled patients in new occupations, the training of doctors, nurses, and medical assistants, and in every way to assist the co-ordination of a comprehensive leprosy service which would bring the benefits of modern treatment to as many patients as possible within easy reach of their homes.

As a result of Dr. Fraser's interest in this new field some quite substantial amounts were granted to various institutions, such as £2,000 for a doctor's house at Ochadamu, £10,000 for buildings at Kumi/Ongino, £10,000 for a new ward and water supply at Shashemane, £8,000 for development at Fiwale Hill, £3,400 for buildings and an airstrip at Luampa, £2,000 for a church building at Chitokoloki, and so on. In this and other ways a good deal of help was given to the work in Africa. A different kind of encouragement was experienced at Kumi when Princess Margaret and her husband honoured the station with a visit. Mrs. Lea describes the occasion:

As you may imagine, the great excitement during the last few months was Princess Margaret's visit. The very day we heard that she would be coming to Kumi my husband confirmed that we had three cases of measles in the school! Of course, we had to report it, and for the next ten days we lived on a see-saw as medical officers of increasing importance visited us to see for themselves how we could organise things so that the Princess ran no risk. Everything was complicated by the fact that we had promised the powers-that-be that our children would be 60 ft. away from the Royal party, and also from the other children, who were sure to flock to see the Princess. Measles in Uganda is a serious disease—some of our children were really very ill, in spite of having my husband and a Children's Sister to look after them with all the help of modern drugs. To risk giving it to children attending day schools from bush homes was out of the question, so long ropes were fixed, isolating the children.

Mrs. Lea says that the significant thing was that no-one cared at all about the leprosy; all the concern was about measles! Of courses there was sense in this. Measles is highly infectious; leprosy is not comparable, for reasons which are only slowly being understood.

The Princess was due to arrive at 8.45 a.m. and she was punctual to the minute. By this time our football field was packed with people and beautiful cars. High-ranking Police Officers; pressmen trying to pin down my husband for news; Ministers of State, our Ambassador from London, Senior Medical Officers, etc. The road was lined with school children, with many Guides and Brownies in places of honour. Our own children, 320 of them, were drawn up behind our band, and a row of staff members waiting to be introduced. Everything went marvellously. The Princess and Lord Snowdon had obviously taken the greatest trouble to read the information which my husband had sent about all the folk to be introduced. So this sort of thing happened: Dr. Lea, 'This is Miss Wiggins, Madam, whose father started leprosy work in Teso District and after whom our school is named'. Princess, 'Oh yes, and it was you who translated the Bible into Atesa, wasn't it?' As soon as all the visitors were seated, the whole school broke into a song of welcome composed by our young singing master. Then the smallest ones did a singing game, and the choir sang the lovely Negro Spiritual *Good News* with enormous gusto, and a squad of lively ten to twelve-year-olds did some exercises and the Guides did a Scottish country dance. At the end, taking no notice of the measles, the Princess and her husband went right round among the children, and also greeted quite a lot of the crowd behind the ropes.

Modernization schemes in India went forward at Naini and Kothara as before, with new projects of this type at Chandkhuri and Chandag. The growing out-patient work in the Faizabad area was more firmly established by the opening of a special out-patient centre at Barabanki, between Faizabad and Lucknow, and there were similar developments at Jhalda near Purulia, in the area served by Naini, and at Vellore and other centres. This part of the work was now growing rapidly, and Wilfrid Russell noted what seemed to him the increasing strain on the staff caused by travel to out-patient clinics at a considerable distance and heavy work on arrival. Calicut received grants for development from a German source. One notable addition to the facilities provided at Purulia was a provision of a much needed community centre. On the wall of this building there was constructed a fine mosaic on the theme 'The Tree of Life', designed by Mr. A. D. Askew. At the end of 1963 Dr. A. T. Roy retired on the completion of 36 years of service with the Mission and so brought to an end his long connection with the medical work at Purulia.

The policy of recruiting missionary personnel was vigorously pursued. Many of those whose names have become well-known in the world of leprosy were appointed in these years.

Expenditure on missionaries had increased by fifty per cent in the previous five years, from £20,000 to £30,000. Even so the Council resolved to continue recruitment to the utmost possible extent. So in 1964 and 1965 there were more appointments. But whereas formerly practically all candidates for missionary service came from the United Kingdom, now the Auxiliaries were beginning to make an important contribution to the ministry of healing by personal service.

The Mission was in fact now building up an increasingly strong missionary team, and this meant more work for those who had responsibility for them. The Committee which had formerly dealt with candidates was now discontinued; and in its place two Committees were appointed—a Candidates Committee for their selection and training, and a Missionary Personnel Committee to deal with the affairs of missionaries 'with special references to emergency situations' which now began to arise from time to time.

The Council had the pleasure of congratulating Dr. C. S. Goodwin on securing the Cambridge M.D. and Dr. E. P. Fritschi on his new qualification, F.R.C.S. (Edinburgh). Other distinctions noted in the Minutes of the Council were the award of the C.B.E. to Dr. Paul Brand in 1961, together with his appointment as Principal of the Christian Medical College, Vellore, the Albert Lasker Award to Dr. Brand in 1960, a high honour bestowed at the 8th World Congress of the International Society for the Rehabilitation of the Disabled, and the award of the O.B.E. to Dr. Stanley G. Browne in the Queen's Birthday Honours List of 1965. But the most interesting item of this kind was surely the one reported in the Mission magazine of 1962:

> H.M. King Frederick IX of Denmark has recently conferred on Miss Emilie Lillelund, S.R.N., the Royal Gold Medal of Merit with Crown of the First Degree in recognition of her services to leprosy sufferers. For thirty years Miss Lillelund of the Danish Missionary Society served with devotion as Superintendent of the Home and Hospital at Vadathorasalur, India, and was rewarded by seeing an extension of its service in many directions.

Bishop H. Fuglsang-Damgaard, the Chairman of the Denmark Auxiliary said of Miss Lillelund:

> She has always shown a real Christian love for the sufferers from leprosy, never sparing herself, inspired as she was by an indefatigable care for bringing help for soul and body in obedience to Christ's commandment. Always ready to serve and to give herself, she fulfilled what she felt to be her vocation. On hearing of the distinction conferred upon her Miss Lillelund said, 'It is not primarily a distinction for me, but for our whole Mission and for all our missionaries'.

Interest in missionaries did not distract attention from the importance of training national workers, and between 1960 and 1965 eight medical scholarships were awarded, one of them to Miss Kiran Das, the daughter of Dr. V. P. Das. Dr. C. K. Job was given study leave to enable him to take up further research work in the United Kingdom and in America, and in England the Council continued to support the Leprosy Study Centre inaugurated by Dr. Robert Cochrane and later directed by Dr. Stanley Browne, who also became Medical Consultant to the Mission in 1965. So in various ways and at different levels the Spreading Tree continued to grow.

There were also two new developments which have still to be mentioned.

In 1964 the Prime Minister of Bhutan invited the Mission to help deal with the leprosy problem in that country, and the Council responded by agreeing to send a Commission to Bhutan to report on the situation. At the next meeting in June the Council was informed that the Prime Minister who had issued this invitation had been assassinated! Nevertheless the invitation had been renewed. In due course the Secretary for Southern Asia, Dr. V. P. Das, Dr. P. J. Chandy, and Mr. A. D. Askew went to Bhutan and reported their findings. The Council accepted in principle their recommendation that the Mission should give help to sufferers from leprosy in Bhutan, but felt that for the time being such help should be on a limited scale 'in view of the uncertain political situation in that part of the world'. The time to advance came later. In the meantime Mr. Askew contributed to the Mission magazine an interesting article on Bhutan:

> The Bhutanese call their country Druk, which means Dragonland, and the King is known as Druk Gyalpo—Dragon King. Until two years ago there were only mule tracks, and the journey from the border to Paro, the administrative centre, took at least six days hard trekking over steep, jungle-covered mountains inhabited by bear, elephant, leeches and other unwelcome companions. Now there is a road, built with incredible skill and hard work by Indian Army engineers and a force of Bhutanese and Nepali labourers. From Phuntsholing this road claws its way up mountain sides, clings to the face of sheer cliffs, and teeters over 9,000 ft. passes, writhing further and further into the country. In places it is simply a scratch on the skin of the hills and is nowhere more than sixteen feet wide. In most places it is much narrower, and in one or two never-to-be-forgotten sections a bare ten feet. At Chapchsa our jeep ploughed slowly through six inches of slimy mud, on the one side a vertical rock face, on the other a drop of two thousand feet. Waterfalls cascade from the mountains and water flows across the road to thunder down the other side in sheets of spray. The road is still unstable and we were told that our journey would take about ten hours, if there were no landslides.

A difficult and even dangerous journey. Was it worth it? Mr. Askew thought it was.

> We finally reached Paro after a day and a half, but it was worth the effort. Driving over hills and through gorges, one enters a narrow valley which gradually widens out from each side of an icy green, freezing cold river, which bounces over a rocky bed down from the high glaciers. This is the Paro Valley, 7,750 feet above sea level. We journeyed up the valley to within thirty miles of the Tibetan border, the country getting wilder and higher all the way. We also went to Thimphu, the capital, thirty miles from Paro, and in another lovely valley, similar to Paro, but at a height

of 8,300 feet and colder. We found more leprosy than expected. There is indeed need for Christian leprosy work in Bhutan, but its form and its scope cannot be decided immediately.

The other growing point of the Spreading Tree proved to be in Ethiopia. In 1964 Paul Brand suggested to the Council that the Mission should co-operate with the International Society for the Rehabilitation of the Disabled in a scheme to establish a Centre at Addis Ababa, the capital of the country, to train local personnel in surgical and rehabilitation techniques. In due course it was learned that some buildings would be available and capital costs would be covered. The contribution of the Mission would be that of personnel to lead the project. The Council agreed to sponsor the provision of a physiotherapist and a doctor or other medical worker. In 1965 Mr. A. D. Askew took part in full discussions in Addis Ababa and finally signed a Memorandum of Association on behalf of the Mission. Mr. Askew explained 'ALERT', the short name of this new enterprise, its full designation being the 'All Africa Leprosy and Rehabilitation Training Centre':

ALERT will be based on the Princess Zenebework Leprosy Hospital at Addis Ababa, which will be taken over and managed by the co-operating Societies as part of the project. Additional buildings will be needed, new wards, workshops, laboratories, physiotherapy and training facilities and staff quarters. The director of the project will be Dr. Felton Ross, who has had a number of years' experience in leprosy work in Nigeria. The Leprosy Mission will be associated with the project in a number of ways, including the provision of a highly skilled physiotherapist, Mr. David Ward, who has worked for eight years at Karigiri, India. The Leprosy Mission has also accepted responsibility for the financial cost of replacing Miss Jane Neville, occupational therapist at Kumi/Ongino in Uganda, who is to be a Church Missionary Society contribution to ALERT. Eventually the project will offer to leprosy patients the techniques of modern medicine and surgery which can bring such hope today but which, so far, are available to only a few of the many sufferers in Africa. Help will not be limited to the hospital. In the surrounding countryside, where the need is so great, an area will be developed so that rehabilitation work can be demonstrated as an integral part of the teaching outreach of the project. 1966 will see the arrival of the first staff members and the completion of a number of essential buildings, and by 1967 it is hoped that the full staff will be working to raise standards in the hospital and to begin work in the control area, so that in the following year there will be the beginning of the teaching ministry.

Through all the ALERT programme we believe that the Christian Church will rise to a new and great challenge in witnessing to the compassion of Jesus through service and teaching.

Chapter Twelve
CONSULTATIONS

THE READER WHO is primarily interested in the actual work of caring for leprosy sufferers may well feel that this chapter can be skipped since it deals largely with the growth and development of the structure of the Mission; nevertheless the process of coming to terms with the need for true internationalism is one which all missionary organizations have to go through. The way it is tackled is of great interest and needs to be understood by the informed supporter of the work.

Turning back to the beginning of the story told in this book, that is to the year 1918, and taking Australia as an example of the older national Auxiliaries, we find that in twenty years from that date—i.e., from 1918 to 1937 inclusive —there were only eight references to the Australian Auxiliary in the Minutes of the Council. There was of course regular correspondence between the General Secretary in London and his colleague in Australia. But at the centre, where decisions were actually being made, the Auxiliary did not seem to have much say in those twenty years. In the last eleven years of the record, 1960 to 1970 inclusive, the picture is quite different. There are fourteen references in the Minutes and several of the later ones refer to discussions of policy on recommendations proposed to the Council by Australia. We have already noted in chapter 10 that in 1959 the Secretary for New Zealand came to London for similar discussions, and in the next few pages we shall see similar approaches made by Denmark and India. Here is the evidence that at the Lucknow Conference of 1953 the national Auxiliaries had become much more aware of themselves than ever before. In these later years the Auxiliaries are increasingly partners in policy-making, rather than merely fund-raising organizations. Consultation at various levels became increasingly significant in the final decade of this part of the Mission's history and a regular feature of the spread of the work.

In Australia Mr. Robert Edgar died in 1963, and Mr. W. R. McKeown succeeded him as Secretary, bringing new vigour to the Auxiliary. Several appointments of Area Secretaries were made here and elsewhere, and in a number of cases Secretaries of Auxiliaries paid visits to the Field to inform themselves about the work at first hand.

In 1961 the Council approved the allocation of £25,000 for projects sponsored by the New Zealand Auxiliary in celebration of its Jubilee, and in 1964 and 1965 the Council agreed to the allocation of funds raised in Denmark, Australia, and New Zealand for schemes recommended by these Auxiliaries, in some cases referring to the financial support of missionaries of co-operating Societies in the countries concerned. In 1965 the Indian Auxiliary requested the services of the Rev. C. M. Lloyd, at this time on the England and Wales deputation staff, to undertake similar work in India. The Council agreed and in due course Mr. and Mrs. Lloyd went out to strengthen the Mission's advocacy in India, particularly in some of the larger city centres. In the same year Scotland elected Dr. R. G. Cochrane Honorary President of the Scottish Auxiliary, and with deep regret recorded the death of Scotland's most senior worker for the Mission, Miss E. MacKerchar, on the 10th November.

She dedicated her life completely to the cause into which God brought her over sixty years ago. In 1904 she became in Edinburgh the first full-time assistant to The Mission to Lepers' Superintendent, Mr. Wellesley Bailey. At once she manifested those qualities which characterized all her service—a meticulous attention to detail, an unfailing enthusiasm, and an utter integrity. In 1917 Miss MacKerchar became the Mission's Secretary for Scotland. As the work grew it came to be divided into areas and she became responsible particularly for the East and the North. When her sisters and brother retired to Fortrose she went North herself and immediately set about building up a stalwart company of supporters in the Highlands and Islands. Official retirement came in 1945, but Miss MacKerchar's enthusiasm in no way abated, and until a few days before her death she remained busily active. With her literary qualifications (she was an L.L.A. of St. Andrew's University) she produced, both before and after her retirement, a number of books for the benefit of the Mission's funds. Her biography of Miss Mary Reed is best known. From the proceeds of her publications buildings for patients were erected at Purulia and Poladpur. Miss MacKerchar's innumerable hand-written letters to subscribers, her annual collection and despatch of many parcels of Christmas articles for patients, her equal attention to the smallest duty and the largest enterprise, all were evidences of her selflessness and the depth of her Christian concern. All she had was at the disposal of her Lord, in forwarding the Mission to which she knew herself to be called.

There is one other item of interest in connection with the Home bases. As preparations began to be made for the proposed meeting of the United Consultative Committee it was realized that England and Wales would be at a disadvantage compared with the remaining Auxiliaries, because whereas they all had their own Councils or Committees with a good deal of autonomy granted to them by their constitutions, England and Wales was represented only by a subcommittee of the Executive Committee of the Council. It was desirable that England and Wales should be put on the same footing as the rest of the Auxiliaries. Accordingly the Council granted England and Wales its own constitution, similar to that enjoyed by other Auxiliaries, and the new Committee for England and Wales was established on 1st January 1962, with Mr. O. Skinner, M.B.E., as Chairman and Mr. G. Newberry Fox as Secretary.

At Headquarters an attempt to promote interest among young people resulted in the appointment of Miss Valerie J. Lawrence in 1961. She gave excellent service, especially in schools, but resigned in 1965. This rather difficult question of the right approach to young people therefore remained still largely unresolved, though deputation secretaries in several countries gave much thought to the problem and achieved some success.

The high professional standing of Dr. Paul W. Brand was recognized by the Council in 1963 when he was formally given Secretarial status, and in the following year, the designation of 'Director of Surgery and Rehabilitation'.

Mr. Bernard Cyril Studd died on March 30th 1962; he was Chairman of the Mission's Council at the time. After describing Mr. Studd's career and his wide range of interest in Christian work and witness (Mr. Studd was for many years Chairman of the British and Foreign Bible Society in Calcutta) Donald Miller continued:

> But it was in Bernard Studd's leadership of the Council of The Mission to Lepers that I came most clearly to see the sterling qualities of this great Christian gentleman. I had known Mr. Studd in India, and when he returned to England he readily responded to the invitation to serve on the Council of the Mission. Immediately it became evident that he had a very special contribution to make, not simply by reason of his experience and ability, but because of a quality of spirit which ensured that every

judgment he made was an out-flowing of his obedience to his Lord. In him there united sweetness and strength, the compassionate heart and the constructive statesman. He gave himself unselfishly to Committee work and in 1953 succeeded Sir Walter Kinnear as Chairman of Council. Thereafter he guided its deliberations with skill and wisdom, always having studied papers so that he was thoroughly versed in whatever was at issue. He gave great encouragement to secretaries, ever at their disposal, never in a hurry. He visited the Field work in India and Hong Kong, and his visits are remembered with gratitude by staff and patients. He had wide vision, and a quiet trust that so long as the Mission was sincerely endeavouring to do its work in the best possible way and reach out to new opportunities, God would bless and provide as had been the case in Korea, Hong Kong, Nepal and elsewhere. Because people mattered so much to him, he always sought to foster and preserve the family spirit in the Mission, rather than engage in mere organizational development. He saw the work essentially as one of the activities of the Household of God, in which we were all family members together, of whatever race or nationality or denomination, engaging in our particular service. To him a man was both man and brother; and Christ was Lord of all.

Sir Harry Greenfield, C.S.I., C.I.E., was elected Chairman in Mr. Studd's place, and in 1963 Sir Paul Benthall, K.B.E., succeeded Sir Maurice Hallett as Honorary Treasurer. In the same year Mr. A. Donald Miller, M.B.E., was elected a Vice-President of the Mission.

At a very early stage in the preparation for the meeting of the United Consultative Committee it was decided that the next Conference should be held at one of the Home bases, and of the various possible countries in which the Conference could meet the most convenient on the whole was the United Kingdom. This was agreed by the Auxiliaries, and it was arranged for Seaview, on the Isle of Wight, in April 1962.

Whereas at Lucknow in 1953 the main emphasis of the Conference was on work directly concerned with leprosy, and the majority of the delegates were engaged in it, the object of the United Consultative Committee was to bring into consultation the representatives of the Home bases and discuss in detail questions relating to their advocacy and any problems that arose in it. For this reason the constitution of the Committee was different from that of the Lucknow Conference. As the Isle of Wight is comparatively near to London there was a stronger representation of the Council of the Mission. The main body of the delegates came from Auxiliaries—Australia two, Canada two, Denmark two, England and Wales two, Hong Kong two, India one, Ireland three, New Zealand two, Scotland two, Southern Africa two and Switzerland one. Special interests were also represented by Dr. Oliver W. Hasselblad, M.D., representing American Leprosy Missions, Inc.; Dr. P. W. Brand, C.B.E., as Director of Orthopaedic Work (as he was then designated); Mr. A. Donald Miller, M.B.E., Vice-President of the Mission; with Dr. P. J. Chandy to speak for India, and the Rev. C. M. Lloyd for Korea. There were also a number of visitors headed by Dr. Robert G. Cochrane, M.D., F.R.C.P., Mr. and Mrs. N. S. Gaze of New Zealand, Mr. J. W. Devonshire of Hong Kong, and the wives of several of the delegates. It was a very representative gathering, and illustrated the wide outreach of the Spreading Tree in support of the primary objective of the Mission, the relief of suffering and the practical expression of Christian compassion.

The Agenda of the Conference exhibited the same broad outlook. At every stage the emphasis was upon consultation, and indeed this word occurs in each of the main headings of the four sections of the Agenda—

A. Consultation on the work of the Supporting Constituencies.
B. Consultation on the relation of the Supporting Constituencies to the Council of the Mission.
C. Consultation on the relation of the Supporting Constituencies to the work on the Field.
D. Consultation on the work of the Mission in relation to Outside Agencies.

Dr. Ernest Muir, C.M.C., C.I.E., was elected Chairman of the Committee.

During the Consultation a good deal of time was spent on the work of the Supporting Constituencies, which was the chief interest of most of the delegates. Here the talk was very down-to-earth, dealing with various aspects of the appeal for funds, such as special projects, supported cases (*i.e.* individual patients or groups of patients supported by donors), 'comforts', literature, audio-visual aids, exhibition material, films and film strips, with special stress on the appeal for personnel in particular and for prayer support in general.

It was in this connection that the Committee asked for time for an addition to the Agenda to enable delegates to consider the use of the word 'Lepers' in the title of the Mission. There was a long and earnest discussion on this subject, as the appropriate resolution of the Committee shows:

A wide variety of views was expressed, but there was a unanimous conviction that there must always be a sensitive concern for those who in any way are likely to suffer more instead of less by reason of the use of the word 'leper'. Some considered that while it was necessary to cut out absolutely the word 'leper' in our speech and literature, there was still a value in retaining at present the title The Mission to Lepers. This was because it emphasizes the fact that millions whom the Mission seeks to serve are still in the condition described by the word 'leper'. On the other hand, some felt it was illogical to cut out the word 'leper' in every other context, but to retain it in the title of the Mission, and pressed for a new name, including the word 'leprosy', but not 'leper'.

This resolution was taken seriously by the Council. In 1964 alternative titles were suggested to the Auxiliaries, and the Chairman of the Council wrote a magazine article on this proposed change in the name of the Mission in which he referred to the view of the United Consultative Committee.

The Committee's recommendations were first examined by the Council and the views of the Mission's eleven Auxiliaries were then sought. Altogether eight possible alternatives were considered and by general consensus the title 'Christian Leprosy Mission' was chosen as complying with the particular exhortation of leading medical opinion, while at the same time preserving both the strong sense of commitment implied in the word 'Mission' and the distinctive Christian quality which has characterized the whole enterprise from its inception. The Council are encouraged to know that American Leprosy Missions, Inc., applaud the proposed title as 'excellent' and 'offer congratulations on what seems to be a very wise choice'. They share our regret in losing a name that has been so honoured and so valued in the whole cause of Christian leprosy work, but suggest that 'surely the name will never really be lost, but only integrated into a larger meaning and purpose'.

At this point the Council was reminded that there existed an organization called the 'International Christian Leprosy Mission' which operated in the U.S.A. and Canada. The Council was advised by the Mission's solicitor, Mr. R. G. Fairbairn, that the similarity of 'Christian Leprosy Mission' to the name of this smaller Society might create legal difficulties, especially in the matter of bequests under the wills of supporters of the Mission. Sir Harry Greenfield then proposed as a solution of the problem the adoption of the simple title 'The Leprosy Mission' and this was accepted at a Special Meeting of Members held in London on the Autumn Day of Fellowship, 2nd October 1965. Henceforward this was recognized as the official title of the Mission. So ended a discussion which had been carried on at intervals over a number of years. The United Consultative Committee had made an important contribution to this debate, and the final action of the Chairman of the Council had given to the Mission the decisive lead which was required at the time, and which he alone could give.

There were other subjects on which the Council took action in response to the recommendations of the United Consultative Committee. One of these was the need for strengthening the link between the Auxiliaries and the Council, and this in fact led to the drafting of a new Constitution of the Mission which would give the Auxiliaries more representation on the Council.

Another suggestion which the Council adopted related to what one delegate called 'areas of special interest'.

The Rev. M. H. Feist (New Zealand) spoke of the interest of New Zealand in the S. Pacific area and the desire to make known the need and relevance of special areas. Southern Africa and Australia had similar situations before them. He thought that the central administration should be unified and free to operate, and it would be harmful to attempt to fractionalise. On the other hand a possible approach to the areas of special interest might be through approved projects to which allocations could be made by the constituencies, with the Council's approval. Several members stressed the need for co-ordination at the centre.

There was also a feeling, strongly expressed by Dr. Hasselblad and Dr. Paul Brand, that The Mission to Lepers (as it was then called) and American Leprosy Missions, Inc. should come much closer together. In resolution 8 of the Committee this view was expressed:

> The Committee was convinced of the value which would accrue if The Mission to Lepers and American Leprosy Missions joined in united planning, financing, and execution of our unfinished task. It therefore resolved to place before the Council the unanimous desire expressed by the representatives of both Missions that the possibility of integration or union between these Missions be explored.

Accordingly a special conference was held in London on March 4th and 5th, 1963. The representatives of the American Society and of the Mission spent two days considering closer co-operation in planning, the extension of the already accepted principal of co-operative budgets, joint action in gathering and producing educational and promotional material, and the need for a detailed co-operative strategy. This was a most helpful consultation, and the two Missions were drawn closer to one another at this time than ever before, but 'integration or union', which the Committee had recommended, was not found to be practicable and was not stressed.

The Council accepted two other proposals of the United Consultative Committee. One of these referred to the continuation of the Committee's work. It was felt that its value had been 'so amply established' that another meeting of the Committee should be held at some time not less than five years and not more than ten years ahead, and in the meantime there should be one or two meetings of the secretaries of the national Auxiliaries to give them the opportunity of consulting with one another and with the Council. This was agreed. The first meeting of National Secretaries was to be held in 1966 and the theme of their Conference would be 'The Changing Pattern in our United Programme'.

The last resolution of the United Consultative Committee spoke of a strong desire to be kept in touch by consultation with Headquarters on matters of common concern and over proposals for development, whether these were put forward by Headquarters or by the Auxiliaries. It was therefore proposed:

> That in view of the extra work that this would involve for the present Headquarters staff there should be the appointment of an additional secretary who would have in mind particularly the needs indicated, together with the encouragement and assistance of the Auxiliaries in building up interest and developing support.

The Council accepted this recommendation and invited the Auxiliaries to make nominations. Three of them responded and after careful consideration the Council appointed Mr. G. Newberry Fox to this new post as 'Promotional Secretary', thus adding a new word to the Mission's official vocabulary and a new idea to the Mission's general policy. Mr. Fox entered on his new duties on July 1st 1963, and the Rev. E. Quintin Snook, a Methodist missionary who had had experience of leprosy work as honorary superintendent of the Raniganj Home was appointed Secretary for England and Wales.

The Promotional Secretary at once began his new task with the same energy he had displayed as Secretary for England and Wales. From 1963 to 1965 he made several visits abroad to make contact with the work on the Field in India, Nepal, and Hong Kong, and with the Auxiliaries in India, Hong Kong, New Zealand and Australia. His main effort, however, was directed towards Europe, a field of support largely untouched (except in Denmark and Switzerland). In his first visit to the Continent in 1963 he went to Valbonne, France, which had not been visited by a Secretary of the Mission for very many years, and met the Rev. Dr. P. C. Toureille, who with his wife was in charge at Valbonne but later entered a wider sphere of service for the Mission.

Mr. Fox found that in France there was some interest in the Mission, but it was looked upon 'as the work of a small British group'. In his report he went on to say that the international character of the Mission was not understood on the Continent and there was considerable surprise when the size and extent of the work was known. There was also some surprise at the fact that this extensive work was not represented on the respective National Protestant Missionary Councils. In the meantime in Germany Dr. Riedel had been able to interest his friends in the work at Chevayur, Calicut, and substantial grants for development at this station were made by the Protestant Central Agency for Development Aid in Bonn. Accordingly the Promotional Secretary followed up this lead, and during his second visit to Europe in the next year he included Germany in his tour programme and made useful contacts at several centres. The possibility of a new field of support also opened up in Holland, and in wider circles in Switzerland and Denmark. It appears that Mr. Newberry Fox found the European situation different from that in the United Kingdom because of the different attitude of the Churches on the Continent to missionary support. Even so he felt that there were sufficient possibilities of development in selected countries in Europe to justify him in asking for funds to promote the advocacy of the Mission in these new areas. The Council agreed to make the necessary financial provision.

The Ninetieth Anniversary of the Mission was celebrated in 1964. The Anniversary celebrations included a special Day of Witness and Intercession, the publication of the history of the Mission up to 1917 written by Mr. A. Donald Miller—*An Inn Called Welcome*—and the issue of an enlarged

Anniversary edition of the Prayer Cycle. The Rev. Walter Fancutt produced an admirable brochure graphically setting out the Mission's story from the 'Desolation and Despair' of the early hopeless leprosy beggars to 'The Search for a Cure' and 'Reaching out to the Sufferers', with details of the world compass of the work at that time. The brochure was introduced by Sir Harry Greenfield's article 'These Ninety Years' and had a wide circulation; 21,000 copies were issued, many of them finding their way to well-wishers outside the usual Mission circles.

Several special projects were adopted as part of the Anniversary. Appeals were made for nine doctors and nine nurses; a large sum was set aside (from the estate of the late Miss Ivy Gibb, of Australia) for a new project in Papua/New Guinea to be undertaken by the Australian Auxiliary in association with New Zealand; and an appeal was made to provide Dr. C. K. Job, who by this time had achieved distinction as a pathologist, with an electron microscope to enable him to carry much further his enquiry into the deeper mysteries of leprosy.

Chapter Thirteen
THE NEAR NORTH

MR. G. NEWBERRY FOX was appointed General Secretary at the March meeting of the Council in 1965 and took over from Wilfrid Russell towards the end of August that year. He had already had considerable experience of the Mission's work, first as a member of the Council from 1944, later as Secretary for England and Wales from 1958, and more recently in the newly created post of Promotional Secretary. He was therefore well equipped for the task to which he applied himself energetically.

The expression 'The Near North' appears in the records

for the first time as far back as 1960, when the New Zealand Council drew attention to the need for leprosy work in this area. Some must have been rather puzzled by the term. Where *was* 'The Near North'? A natural question for those who live in the West, but clearly answered when it is realized that what Europeans call the Far East is to colleagues in Australia and New Zealand the great area lying to their north, and very much closer to them than the Mission's work in India or Africa. So because of this concern of these two Auxiliaries the interest of the Mission was now aroused in Papua/New Guinea first of all, and then in Indonesia—two new fields for the Mission.

The Papua/New Guinea scheme developed quite rapidly. One reason was that funds were available for the extension of the Mission's work in the area, and personnel also responded to the new challenge. The estate of the late Miss Ivy Gibb provided the former, and the vigorous advocacy of the Secretaries of Australia and New Zealand in their own countries soon began to produce the dedicated and skilled workers which the new enterprise would require. The challenge to them was certainly great, as many friends of the Mission must have realised when they heard Mr. W. R. McKeown, Secretary for Australia, speak so enthusiastically about an area of which they knew very little.

The Australian Territory of Papua and the Trust Territories of New Guinea are combined in an administrative unit comprising the eastern part of New Guinea and many hundreds of lesser islands. Papua has an area of 86,100 square miles. It became a British possession in 1888 and was handed over to Australia in the year 1906. New Guinea has an area of 92,160 square miles and was a German possession until the 1914-1918 war. Then Australia was made repsonsible for its administration, first under mandate from the League of Nations, and now, since 1946, under United Nations Trusteeship. Papua/New Guinea is a rugged country, very mountainous, with many rivers. It is a truly stone-age society emerging into a modern world. Today, it is seeking its independence, largely due to outside pressures. The indigenous Melanesian population is made up of over two million people, and the European, Asian, and other mixed-blooded peoples make up about 28,000 inhabitants of the Territories.

Mr. McKeown admitted that as an Auxiliary of the Mission Australia had not previously faced its responsibilities in regard to these Territories and had not realized how much leprosy was to be found there. This was discovered when visits were made by Dr. N. D. Fraser, Dr. Paul Brand, and Dr. Grace Warren, and there was a thorough investigation into the leprosy situation. Mr. McKeown then went on to say:

> There are thirteen leprosy centres in Papua/New Guinea with thirteen individual Missionary Societies working among leprosy sufferers. After an initial survey the Missions were all brought together for consultation. With a new enthusiasm they accepted the views of experts as to what could be done, determined to do all in their power to accomplish the end in view. A Government surgeon, a physiotherapist from New Zealand and a theatre sister who commenced her work in England, were trained at Karigiri as the first surgical unit team. The very day after they landed in New Guinea they operated on eight cases of leprosy and in a period of nine months they carried out over 500 operations on hands, feet, and faces.

As news of the work spread through the hills and valleys, sufferers from leprosy began to pour in, and the work therefore had to expand to meet the growing need:

> A further Government worker was sent to India for training as an orthopaedist and is now back in New Guinea teaching others how to make the very necessary remedial footwear. The people he has trained will be able to go out into all the various parts of Papua/New Guinea ensuring that footwear is available. Now, as a further expansion of the work the Mission is to have a second team trained for its own surgical work. Dr. W. Ramsay and his wife, who is also a doctor, are being trained at Karigiri for this forward-looking work.

This was in 1966, and still the work grows. By 1968 the Council learned that since a base had been established at Tari 'great advance had been made', and over 37,000 cases had been surveyed in the Southern Highlands. The General

Secretary had also visited Papua/New Guinea.

Since Tari has already been mentioned, and also Dr. Ramsay, it may be of interest to record his early impressions of this station on taking up work there after his special training at Karigiri. First a more general statement:

Having visited nine leprosy institutions in this Territory, two major impressions stand out in my mind. The first is that the number one problem throughout the Territory is the prevention of the destruction of feet. This is not surprising, since the lack of suitable footwear for leprosy patients has meant that any attempts to heal ulcers are bound to end in recurrence and disappointment. I am glad to say that the outlook is more promising now with shoe material to hand and satisfactory patterns being worked out.

The second is that any leprosy work which does not include a control programme to deal with the root of the disease is like trying to bale out a boat without repairing the leak. Much good work is being done by different Missions and the Administration under conditions that are, at times, far from ideal.

Dr. Ramsay goes on to speak of Tari, a station operated for many years by one of the Australian Missionary Societies.

It is not difficult to see the many advantages of Tari as our centre of activity rather than any of the other centres in the Highlands. The standard of work and patient-care here in past years compares very favourably with any I observed elsewhere. This is a real community and the way the patients are willing to co-operate with the staff and help each other reflects the happy nature of the Huli people, and the depth of Christian love and service that has been fostered by the workers of the Methodist Overseas Mission. The facilities in the hospital here should be quite adequate for the programme that is planned. The two wards in the surgical block, with 12 beds, should provide accommodation for surgical cases and any seriously ill patients, and they have already been pressed into service. The remainder of the patients live in indigenous type houses with about twelve patients in each. Although my first thoughts were in favour of Western-style wards there are real advantages in having the patients live in the style they will go back to after discharge. This way of life is the one in which they must learn to care for themselves, so it is desirable to teach them to live safely in their own type of dwelling.

Dr. Ramsay's report was headed 'Open Doors in Papua/New Guinea'. Even more dramatic was the challenge of an open door set before the Mission for entry into a new field in Indonesia. This was first described at a meeting of National Secretaries held at Hildenborough Hall, Otford, prior to the General Council of 1968; we quote from the published report:

> The Rev. Murray H. Feist (Secretary for New Zealand) and Mr. W. R. McKeown (Secretary for Australia) have recently carried out an extensive survey tour of Indonesia and their reports were stimulating and full of challenge. Indonesia is made up of 3,000 islands, running from West Irian (formerly W. New Guinea) to Sumatra. It has a total area of 735,000 square miles and a population of 106,000,000. There is a good deal of leprosy in Indonesia, with much deformity, due to lack of medical treatment, physiotherapy, and surgery. After conferring with Government Health leaders and missionary workers, the Mission's representatives recommend that, with the co-operation of Government and Missions, a specialist group of workers should be recruited, including a surgeon, a physiotherapist, a theatre sister, and a business manager. The Mission would use as base a leprosy settlement at Sitanala, about 16 miles from Jakarta, and the new work would be similar to that undertaken by the Mission's team at present operating in Papua/New Guinea. Besides the work of surgical reconstruction and social rehabilitation, it is also planned to use leprosy control methods in the areas of greatest need seeking early cases and offering treatment on the widest possible scale. The 1962 survey of leprosy in Indonesia gave a total of 49,690 registered cases with an estimated 124,000 cases requiring treatment. The Leprosy Mission's aid will therefore be greatly appreciated by Government leprologists and missionary workers already tackling Indonesia's leprosy problems.

This general programme was approved, and the Councils of Australia and New Zealand were given authority to direct it through the Secretary of the Australian Auxiliary as the

Mission's representative in Indonesia. Many members of the audience at the Annual General Meeting of that year must have been surprised to hear of an 'open door' of opportunity in a country like Indonesia, which has a predominantly Muslim population, but after discussions with officials assurances had been given that there would be freedom for a spiritual ministry by a Christian Mission, even though there might be local opposition. An agreement with the Government of the Republic of Indonesia was actually signed in April 1969. Work began at Sitanala as planned, and by 1970 Dr. Ernest Fritschi had arrived from India to lead the surgical team.

Another 'area of special interest', as Mr. Feist would call it, was Thailand, which was also visited by the Secretaries of Australia and New Zealand. Through their advocacy the Council of 1968 authorized a plan to augment, direct, and finance the leprosy surgery and control group at Chiengmai, a well-known centre supported for many years by American Leprosy Missions, and at Manorom, which had received help from The Leprosy Mission. Mr. Alan Davis made a survey of need in the Manorom area and of the possibilities of development there, and his main recommendations received support from Dr. Stanley Browne when he visited Thailand. The Council made grants for this control scheme, both for capital outlay and for maintenance of the work, the American Society sharing the cost. Perhaps the most significant contribution to the development of the work in Thailand was made by the Australian Auxiliary. By 1970 the Secretary was able to report to the Council that no fewer than seven Australian staff members had been appointed to work at Chiengmai.

Other schemes went steadily forward, if not with the same impetus as the new ventures just described. In Nepal plans were laid for phased development of the work based on Anandaban, and a grant was made in support of the Robert Edgar Memorial Ward project. The Mission gave help to the Nepal Evangelistic Band in the construction of their new leprosy hospital at Pokhra, bearing the delightful name of 'Green Pastures'. In 1968 the Medical Consultant of the Mission was officially invited to visit Nepal for a conference on leprosy at which the World Health Organization, the Government of Nepal, and the Missions concerned would discuss future policy for leprosy work in the country. One of the results of this helpful consultation was the formation of the Nepal Leprosy Relief Association, to which Dr. Johs Andersen was invited to act as technical adviser.

The General Secretary was greatly encouraged by what he saw when he visited Kathmandu in 1969. He said that he found the work, now under the leadership of Dr. John Harris, facing 'tremendous opportunities', particularly with the possibility of making a practical approach to local need in the Lele Valley nearby. Dr. J. C. Pedley's fine work at Tansen, in association with the United Mission to Nepal and with Government at a high level, was also deserving of praise, especially his enterprise in striking out in new research. Dr. Pedley visited Afghanistan in 1969 to investigate the leprosy situation and presented an interesting and encouraging report. The next year the Medical Assistance Programme, which was in charge of medical work in that country, approached the Mission for help, and a grant was made by the Council.

Bhutan had by now ceased to be as remote as it was. Dr. and Mrs. Riedel had done magnificent pioneer work and negotiations were soon in hand for the building of a hospital at Gida Kom, near Thimphu. In due course Dr. Riedel and his wife went home on leave and Dr. and Mrs. J. S. Berkeley took up the work, particularly that of survey of new villages in areas of endemicity.

In India the outstanding advance in this period was made at Salur, where Dr. Thangaraj had been enthusiastically engaged in the work which his father had directed many years before. In association with the Lutheran World Federation a plan was submitted for a new hospital and subsidiary buildings at a cost of about £45,000, of which the Mission and American

Leprosy Missions were asked to find half, and the Lutheran Mission to find the other half. Several grants were made by the Council between 1967 and 1970 and the Salur scene was transformed. In this connection, the United Christian Youth Committee of Sutton Coldfield, England, raised the sum of £5,607.

Its chairman was a young enthusiast whose name comes into The Leprosy Mission picture in a different connection later— John Geater. The money was to be devoted to the Rehabilitation and Orthopaedic Centres at Salur and Vizianagram, where Dr. (Mrs.) Thangaraj was in charge, and the new Artificial Limb Centre at Salur was opened on September 17th, 1970. Many other large projects were financed—in 1966 a special research project for Karigiri and Vellore; in 1967 the Muzaffarpur hospital, an orthopaedic workshop at Karigiri, a doctor's house at Jhalda, near Purulia, and another at Vadathorasalur, an out-patient block at Narsapur, and the third stage of the modernization scheme at Chandag; in 1968 more grants for Muzaffarpur and a special maintenance grant of over £3,000 for Kothara, where the Government grant-in-aid had been withdrawn for a time; in 1969 an administration block at Karigiri and staff quarters at Miraj; finally in 1970 £6,422 for a ward and staff houses at Barabanki, near Faizabad, to meet the continuing demands of out-patient work. There were also many smaller grants.

It was decided that the small Home at Dhar should be closed and the few remaining patients were transferred elsewhere. Thought was given to the salary levels of Indian workers to enable them to meet a sharp rise in the cost of living, and steps were taken for the setting up of Indian Leprosy Mission Trusts to hold Mission property in the three main regions of India. Discussion with American Leprosy Missions of a new constitution for the Schieffelin Leprosy Research Sanatorium at Karigiri took place to define more precisely its nature, and relationship with the Mission and with the Christian Medical College at Vellore. The Secretary for Southern Asia was authorized to look for a site at New Delhi for the India office of the Mission; it seemed desirable (and indeed had been suggested years before) that this office should now be situated close to the centre of Government; it was in fact much later established at the capital city.

Both the official records of the Mission and pubilicity material issued about this time are so much concerned with the two new Fields in 'the near North' and with development in general that references to individual patients are noticeably fewer. But there are still a few, such as the story of Napha of Palampur in Himachal Pradesh—that is to say, in the foothills of the Himalayas.

The news passed round the Leprosy Home at Palampur and many wept openly when they heard it. 'Napha is dead.' Only three words, but for many this spelled thirty years, for that is the length of time Napha had lived in the Leprosy Home, and when he died at seventy-five years of age he was the oldest patient at Palampur.

When he was sixty-four years of age he began to lose his sight, and it was a great sorrow to him when he found he could no longer read the Scriptures he had learnt to love. It was suggested that at Ludhiana Medical College there were surgeons who might be able to give him back his sight. His reply was typical of his courage. After thinking for a little while he said, 'I expect it will be very costly.' 'Oh yes,' was the answer, 'it will be costly, but you need not worry about that, for money will be found to meet your every need.' Napha's face was grave as he quietly answered, 'Then I shall not go to Ludhiana. You must find some younger man and let him have the operations in my place. I am getting an old man and am so fortunate to have so much of God's Word in my heart. If there is a younger man who is going blind it will mean so much more to him if he regains his sight'. Napha's wishes were fulfilled and another patient was given the care and treatment he might have had, but in Napha's heart there was much joy and the eye of faith gave him sight which could not be taken away.

One is tempted to add by way of comment John Bunyan's couplet:

> *Who would true valour see,*
> *Let him come hither.*

Another sidelight on Christian teaching, this time from a very different angle, is contributed by Mr. John Ayers, of Faizabad. He was crossing the compound of the Children's Sanatorium one night, and heard the sound of voices:

> Coming to quarter No. 2 I listened, thinking that perhaps I might discover some plotted mischief. But three voices were discussing faith. 'In my village Ram "walks",' said the first voice, 'and sometimes Lord Krishna.' 'Yes,' said a second boy, 'Lord Krishna "walks" in my village but we also have a Muslim mosque.' Thoughtfully a third voice came in. 'But in this hospital, here, Jesus Christ "walks".' And, as an afterthought, 'I have heard that He also "walks" in the Punjab.' Nothing more was said, so I coughed and asked why the light was still burning. There was a scuffle, and the three dived for their plank beds. I asked them if they did not think that Jesus was in their home villages also. No, they had never heard of Him; never heard His name, or even of His Church. Only by contracting leprosy had they come into contact with the healer of mankind. The conclusion was therefore that it was proper to worship Jesus here, and at home Ram or Krishna, for accepting the Lord Jesus Christ destroys the security of home and family. To become a Christian is to become an outcast again.

What would the reader of this chapter say in reply to this sample of schoolboy logic?

The Hong Kong situation was rather different from that in India. The number of resident patients at Hay Ling Chau was now falling steadily. With provision for 540 beds the number of patients in 1969 was 281, and the figure tended to decline still further. This did not mean lack of success in the anti-leprosy campaign, but rather the reverse. The Hong

Kong Government had successfully established and maintained out-patient treatment in clinics, and the pressure on Hay Ling Chau had therefore been eased. This helped to release Dr. Grace Warren and Miss Jean Watson for the valuable assistance and guidance they were able to give in surgery and physiotherapy at other centres in the Far East.

On an earlier page Miss Batstone has described the beauty of the approach to the island, and particularly that of the jetty with its welcoming air and its flame-coloured flowering trees. But it could also be a place of sadness for some.

> The Wednesday morning arrival of the *Ling Hong* with its quota of new patients and their relatives is a constant reminder of the anguish which leprosy brings to patients and their families; the anguish of parting from loved ones; the anguish of the stigma which now attaches to the entire family; the anguish, sometimes, of learning that one has passed on the disease to one's loved ones.
>
> Consider, for example, the Leung family. I was down at the jetty one Wednesday morning meeting new patients, among whom was a little nine-year-old girl accompanied by her brother. As we gathered to talk under the flame trees I noticed out of the corner of my eye that one of the patients, who are always around when new patients arrive, had started to weep quietly to herself. Was she, I enquired, a relative? Not according to our records, I was told. Later that day the truth came out. She was the girl's mother, but had previously concealed from us that she had this daughter. She seems to have been down at the jetty that day quite by chance, only to endure the double shock of seeing her daughter admitted as a patient and of knowing that she herself must have infected her. Another cruel blow came two weeks later, when her eleven year old daughter was also admitted. The girls now play happily, the mother is a little less wan and sad; we can only imagine the feelings of the remaining family in Hong Kong.

Mr. S. J. Viner, a member of the England and Wales staff, made a generous offer to work in Korea, and in 1967 he and his wife went out to serve for about three years. The pattern of the Korean work was changing as the village clinics established by Mr. Lloyd and Miss Bennett began to be absorbed into the Government Health Service. The Mission had first shown a new way to deal with leprosy in the villages, and Government was now beginning to follow the lead which the Mission had given. In 1970 the authorities of the Taegu University Hospital offered a five-year extension of the agreement, dating from 1972, and the Executive Committee of the Mission responded favourably to this invitation. In the meantime excellent work continued to be done by Miss Grace Bennett and Miss Patricia Hunn, as Mr. Alan Waudby found when he visited Korea as the Mission's Representative in the Far East.

The African scene in these five years 1965 to 1970 exhibited a pattern of light and shade. On the sunnier side of the picture the ALERT project in Ethiopia was more firmly established. Dr. C. S. Goodwin joined the staff, with special responsibility for the treatment of patients and supervision of the laboratory. He returned to England in 1969 and in his place a Korean doctor was appointed for whom the Mission provided support. In 1968 the project was greatly honoured by the presence of the Emperor of Ethiopia, who laid the foundation stone of the Princess Zenebework Leprosy Hospital in Addis Ababa and paid tribute to the organizations which had co-operated to make the ALERT scheme viable. A magazine article entitled 'A Royal Occasion' gives some details of the project:

The new leprosarium is to be the centre of a training programme which will greatly affect leprosy work throughout the entire continent. Among members of The Leprosy Mission on the staff are Dr. C. S. Goodwin (bacteriologist), Mr. D. J. Ward (physiotherapist), and Mr. P. E. Hill (orthopaedic appliance maker). Other members of the international team working on the ALERT scheme at Addis Ababa are Dr. W. Felton Ross (Director of Training), Dr. M. Fitzherbert (physician), Dr. Luther Fisher (orthopaedic surgeon), Miss J. Neville (ocupational therapist) and the Rev. Daniel Sensenig (Business Manager). If this seems a formidable team it has to be remembered that there are still a number of senior posts to be filled if the ALERT scheme is to offer the kind of specialized training in leprosy care and control which is required in view of Africa's leprosy problems. The new 100-bed hospital will have X-ray, laboratory, and pharmacy departments besides housing the administration offices and research institute. In addition to the regular training courses which are planned, the ALERT centre will provide facilities for conferences of doctors, nurses, and others who are dealing with leprosy in Africa, and in the future working of the centre lies the hope of leprosy control and its possible eradication in the African continent. Mr. A. D. Askew, Assistant General Secretary of The Leprosy Mission, was able to attend the stone-laying ceremony for the new hospital block and was afterwards presented to His Imperial Majesty Haile Selassie I. Later, Mr. Askew was able to evaluate the work being done by The Leprosy Mission's representatives and also to attend the official annual meeting of the Board of Directors of ALERT.

His Imperial Majesty also paid a short visit to Shashemane. His arrival was 'a little muddled' through excess of enthusiasm, as this account shows:

We had prepared very carefully for our visitor, with decorations of flowers and an arch topped by a crown and cut-out words of greeting. He went all round the compound and we had an exhibition of hand-crafts done by the patients. His arrival was a little muddled by the landing of a big helicopter in the field at the side of the compound. All the children, thinking that the Emperor was arriving by helicopter, went tearing down to the gate to be sure to greet him, with teachers streaming after them to bring them back. Just as they were rushing out on to the road, His Imperial Majesty's car drove in! The helicopter was being piloted by the head of the Ethiopian Air Force, who, seeing all the flags and the parade, then the approaching royal car, didn't want to miss the fun, so landed to get in on it! What a word of warning that was. The wholehearted preparation for the Emperor's coming—as little Beshadu said, 'This is how we should prepare for the coming of the Lord Jesus.' All these folk went tearing off to see the helicopter, thinking that the Emperor was in it, and then were taken unawares when he did come. So many people are side-tracked with other things, so busy here and there, or perhaps following some new 'Gospel', that when the Lord Jesus comes, they will be caught unawares and be unready.

Mr. Peter Hill spent two years at the Oji River Settlement in Nigeria, his object being to train Nigerian workers in his own special skills:

My job was to set up an Orthopaedic Workshop, training Nigerians to make shoes, braces for legs and splints for hands. Although there was not much of a workshop to start with, the men had already learned something of the art of making artificial limbs, and they were doing it quite well, but they had only two machines to work with, a sewing machine and a grinder. The first thing that had to be done was to teach the men normal methods of workshop practice, tidiness and careful handling of machines and tools, etc. The first workshop was very small, and after about a year we moved into a larger building. During the first twelve months my time was mainly spent in teaching the men simple leather work. We had ordered tools and equipment but these things always take about twelve months to arrive, so it was a long time before we could get down to real work. Then, of course, there was the matter of finding the money to pay for the tools and materials, but God provided in many wonderful ways. After a year the workshop began to take shape and even looked really efficient! The men had already been making a simple sort of shoe, but this wasn't really suitable for the prevailing conditions, and didn't last long. So we designed a shoe that would last for a year, even with hard wear. This was only a beginning. There were many improvements made to the design of artificial legs, and many different types of appliances to be used by the leprosy patients. The men in the workshop were very keen, most of them very hard-working, and their main ambition was to learn. Much of my time was spent in moulding them together as a team, instilling into them the idea of doing a good job and having a real love for the patients with whom they were dealing. Mr. Hill and his wife and family left for home leave in October 1966 and hoped to return to Oji River. This was not possible because the deep shadow of Civil War had now fallen upon Eastern Nigeria, and Mr. Hill was therefore posted to the ALERT project in Addis Ababa, as we have seen.

The records of this period give some information about the situation in Nigeria, but not as much as one would wish. Here is an interim report:

Early in the war the Church of Scotland Leprosy Hospital at Itu was bombed and almost completely destroyed. Some leprosy centres were over-run by the warring forces and the fate of patients is not known for certain. Some managed to get to refugee camps but there is no medicine available for them, and little food. One doctor speaks of patients 'crawling on hands and knees . . . scarecrows . . . skin and bone'. Hundreds of needy patients trekked, when they had sufficient strength, from centre to centre seeking the little medicine and food available. The death rate from malnutrition, famine, and untreated disease adds up to a proportion which it is sickening to envisage and the outlook is grim indeed unless the war ends soon. Even so, it will be too late for many thousands of innocent sufferers. Missions and charities are accumulating food, drugs, and other supplies pending the opening up of supply-corridors but, when peace does come, the need for the re-establishment of leprosy work must make considerable demands upon our resources and we must be ready to act as soon as action is possible. Meanwhile we are doing all we can, in conjunction with co-operating Missions and others, to alleviate human suffering wherever possible.

A later statement said:

Among the co-operating Missions hardest hit by the war in Nigeria is the Qua Iboe Mission, whose leprosy centres have been supported by The Leprosy Mission for many years. For the first time in the history of the Qua Iboe Mission most of their area of operation is without missionaries. A few months ago all but seven of the missionaries in the Western Region had left Nigeria and arrangements were in hand to withdraw the remainder. The advancing Federal forces engulfed the area of Etinan while five of the Q.I.M. missionaries were together in Ikot Okoro hospital compound. They dutifully surrendered to the Federal Commander and, after four weeks' detention in Calabar, were repatriated to the United Kingdom. Another co-operating Society, the Church Missionary Society, announced with deep regret the murder of two of its senior missionaries in Nigeria, Mr. and Mrs. A. F. C. Savory, who had returned with a relief team. We offer our sympathy to the bereaved relatives and give thanks to Almighty God for the faithful service of our friends who have laid down their lives in the country of their adoption.

A joint Committee was formed to plan for reconstruction of leprosy work in Nigeria following the cessation of hostilities, and the Mission set aside £10,000 for this purpose. Dr. Stanley Browne was officially invited to undertake a survey of the leprosy problem in the East Central State of Nigeria and Mr. A. Hasted was asked to study the needs of Uzuakoli, but at the end of 1970 the situation was still somewhat obscure. What is certain is that a very fine piece of leprosy work in this part of Nigeria had been gravely harmed, and it would take a long time to heal the wounds of war.

Another area of conflict during this period was the Sudan; there is very little information about the sufferings of the Sudanese during that time. But there is at least one reference to a refugee from this unhappy country. It occurs in a report sent in by Dr. Edward H. Williams, M.B.E., of the Africa Inland Mission Hospital at Kuluva, Uganda:

Every day the nurse goes the rounds of our leprosy settlement to see the patients, supervise their medical dressings and so on. One of them, John, is a Sudanese refugee, and when he came to us he was unable to walk. For days he had crawled as best he could, and when he crossed the border a friendly African official picked him up and brought him to us. He informed us that most of his family had been shot during the disturbances in his country. We treated his ulcers by putting his feet in plaster and we hope to have him walking again soon.

In sharp contrast to all this Mr. George Hart, the indefatigable and resourceful Farm Manager at Hombolo, reported 'plenteous harvests' of grain, and much progress in various branches of the work, now in its seventh year.

This sort of encouragement comes to us, he says, from time to time enabling us to believe that in our medical and spiritual work, as on our farm, 'we shall reap, if we faint not'.

On September 14th 1965 a great man died whose name was known all over the world. Since 1951 the Mission had regularly supported Dr. Albert Schweitzer's leprosy work at Lambarene in Gabon. It was therefore desirable that when the Assistant General Secretary made his next visit to this part of the world he should give some time to Lambarene. He found Dr. Van Joost co-operative and ready to undertake improvements in the organization of the leprosy village and the treatment given to patients. Mr. Askew recommended the development of a programme for physiotherapy and surgery, and suggested that the Mission might help.

On the medical front the outstanding event of this period was the installation of the electron microscope which had been one of the 1964 Ninetieth Anniversary projects. The scheme had strong support from the medical advisers of the Mission and there was a generous response from the public. After much consideration it was decided that the miscroscope should be installed at the Christian Medical College, Vellore, in a specially constructed air-conditioned room, and it was here that the valuable instrument was dedicated by Bishop Lesslie Newbigin on July 18th 1966.

Dr. C. K. Job indicated ways in which electron-microscopy would help in further study of leprosy. He said the first idea of the project came to him when he was on study-leave in England. In Oxford and London he had been able to see the work of men like Dr. G. Weddell, the famous neuro-anatomist, and he was sure that lines of study they were pursuing would be a great advantage in S. India where facilities for such study were so good owing to the research already done at Karigiri and Vellore. Leprosy, said Dr. Job, is a mysterious disease. No-one yet knows how the disease is transmitted from one person to another. So many questions await an answer. Is it primarily a Schwann cell disease? Where are the bacilli located in the nerve at the early stage of the disease? The answers, if we can find them, could be most fruitful.

Miss Gillian Douglas, a technician highly qualified in electron microscopy, was seconded by the Church Missionary Society to assist Dr. Job in his research. A number of important scientific papers have already been issued, written for the most part in language so technical that for the ordinary reader quotations might prove more mystifying than helpful. Already Dr. Job has made good use of the powerful instrument which modern science has placed in his hands.

Another addition to the doctor's armament in his fight against leprosy was the new drug B663, already briefly mentioned in chapter 9. Dr. Vincent Barry, of Trinity College, Dublin, whose researches along with those of his team produced this new drug in the laboratories of the Irish Medical Research Council, has spoken of the long study which culminated in the production of the drug, an interesting example of the endless patience of the dedicated research worker:

> About twenty years ago, following a lead which we got when we were investigating some substances which occur in a lichen which grows commonly on walls by the sea in County Dublin, we extracted a substance that started us on a synthetic programme, ending up with a red drug which we called B283. Dr. Barnes, who was working in Uzuakoli, Nigeria, tried it out on a small number of leprosy patients and they were delighted with it. They called it 'the King of Drugs', though it was somewhat toxic and added to their discomfort, so it was obviously not the answer. However, it was a start in this particular line and we continued investigations with this type of substance until we eventually arrived, in 1957, with B663.

In the following decade further field trials were carried out, side by side with laboratory investigations:

> It has become clear that B663 (now given the name Lamprene) is a drug of great value, healing leprosy lesions

at the same time as it destroys the bacilli causing the disease. At the same time, also, the new drug is able to suppress the dangerous reaction—the lepra reaction, as we have come to call the condition—which has brought so much distress to certain leprosy patients under care. Patients, some of whom have been ten to sixteen years in reaction, have responded promptly to the new drug and, as the reaction has subsided, they have begun to feel well, to be free from pain and have entered 'a new and cheerful view of existence'.

Dr. Grace Warren made a similar report on the use of the drug in her work at Hay Ling Chau. As controlled clinical trials of the drug take place in the main leprosy centres throughout the world more complete evidence will be available of the usefulness of B663. Meanwhile, we are grateful to God that He has enabled scientists and leprologists to co-operate once more in work that brings relief and hope to those whose leprosy has proved so intractable in the past.

A number of scholarships were awarded to medical students in India during the period 1965 to 1970, and in 1967 Dr. Job was given an opportunity to visit Carville in the U.S.A. and Edinburgh in Scotland for further study in electron microscopy. In 1970 his eminence in leprosy research was recognized when he had the honour of being elected a Fellow of the Indian Academy of Medical Science. A new departure was the acceptance by the Council of the principle of awarding scholarships in administrative training, an aspect of the work now of growing importance, on the same kind of basis as the award of medical scholarships. The first student to receive this award was Mr. Anil Das, the son of Dr. Victor Das, to enable him to take a course in England.

At the request of the American Public Health Service Dr. Paul Brand was attached for a time to the staff of the large leprosy hospital at Carville, Louisiana, to lead a research project to study ways of preventing deformity to hands and feet. He was ably supported by his wife, Dr. Margaret Brand, who had charge of the eye clinic. It is gratifying that Dr. Brand's work was officially recognized by the American Association of Plastic Surgeons in the presentation of a medal of honour for his work on reconstructive surgery, the highest award which this Association could confer. Dr. Brand also received in 1968 the Barclay Medal awarded by the Asiatic Society of America in recognition of his work in India. Dr. Stanley G. Browne was also honoured by the award of the Royal Africa Society's medal, Dr. R. G. Cochrane was congratulated on receiving the C.M.G. and Dr. Katharine Young the O.B.E., both in 1969. Another prominent worker, whose service was mentioned in an earlier chapter, died in 1968, and many people in India, and indeed further afield, received with deep regret news of the death of Dr. W. S. Robertson, F.R.A.C.S., O.B.E., in New Zealand.

After his retirement (from his distinguished career in his own country) in 1954 and at the age of 66, Dr. Robertson volunteered for honorary service with The Mission to Lepers (as it then was) in India. He worked for two years in various centres, notably Karigiri, Faizabad, Purulia, and Chandag, taking part in operations for crippled patients and in preventive and rehabilitation work. Through his work in India he made a distinct contribution to rehabilitation by developing special footwear to protect the anaesthetic feet of the patients. The work was so successful that it changed the pattern of hospital and clinical treatment and it has since been followed by the manufacture and use of this footwear in many countries. In India prejudice decrees that shoe-making is an occupation only suitable for the lower classes, hence it constantly amazed Indians that the Doctor was willing to stoop to such a lowly occupation for the good of the patients. Always transparently sincere, Dr. Robertson expressed his Christianity in deeds rather than words. His was a sensitive spirit so that he felt deeply for people in need and throughout his life he had warm affection for children.

At the General Council of 1969 Dr. Stanley Browne reported on the work of the Leprosy Study Centre in London and discussed medical policy in general. He thought that the future pattern might be one of diversification, a concept of comprehensive medical care, no longer thinking of leprosy alone but also of the whole man in his environment.

The striking feature of this period, and indeed of the whole decade 1960 to 1970, however, was the great increase in out-patient work. The statistics published each year were always to some extent incomplete because of the difficulty of collecting figures from so large a number of co-operating Societies, but even so it was clear that the Spreading Tree was indeed spreading 'wider and wider yet' as the outreach to the patient in his village became more and more effective. Indeed, so much so that the Annual Report for the year ended 31st December, 1970, *Sing Praise to God,* indicated that the total number of out-patients treated must have been at least 150,000, and probably many more. At this point it is perhaps appropriate to quote the two lines of verse from which the title of this book was taken:

Now God be thanked so many stand
In shade of this wide-spreading tree.

As for the policy underlying this outreach, and particularly the concept of domiciliary treatment, that is to say the treatment in village clinics of patients living in their own homes, here is the first paragraph of the Southern Asia section of that Report:

In recent years a silent revolution has been taking place in the world of leprosy. From the introduction of the widespread use of sulphones and the hope of cure which this has brought, has come a change in outlook that affects the whole approach to leprosy. The static treatment of patients in 'Homes' has given way to the dynamic of a new outreach which seeks to meet sufferers where they are; in their village homes, in their comunities, working within the society of which they are members. In other words in homes, not Homes.

One wonders what Wellesley Bailey would have thought of this new idea—'not Homes, but homes'?

The rapid extension of out-patient work led to the training and deployment of an increasing number of paramedical workers and to the continuance of the policy of recruiting missionaries in spite of rising costs.

Looking through the names of those who joined the staff during this period, two points call for comment. One is the wide variety of skills offered by these candidates for missionary service; the other is their background. Whereas in earlier days nearly all offers of missionary service came from young people in the United Kingdom, by the end of the decade under review the Auxiliaries were bringing forward candidates from many countries. The Spreading Tree was becoming more and more truly international in character.

Chapter Fourteen
GENERAL COUNCIL

AT THE MEETING of the United Consultative Committee in 1962 the Auxiliaries had requested more representation on the central Council of the Mission, and accordingly a new Constitution was drafted and submitted to the Auxiliaries for opinion. It was intended that membership of the Mission should be worldwide, and the Council, which would hereafter be known as the General Council, would include the greater representation desired by the Auxiliaries. The General Council would lay down policy, entrusting administrative detail to the Executive Committee, which would meet monthly. The General Council would meet annually, to pass in review the whole work of the Mission, and not quarterly, as the Council had met for so many years. This was essential in view of the considerable travel costs involved in bringing together representatives of the Auxiliaries from as far apart as Canada and New Zealand.

For the same reason it seemed desirable to precede the meetings of the General Council by holding conferences of National Secretaries at Hildenborough Hall, a centre conveniently near London, and time these meetings for early May in each year so that these Secretaries and other overseas members of the General Council could take part in the Annual Meeting of Members of the Mission and the Annual Public

Meeting. The new arrangement was formally approved at a Special Meeting of Members held on 1st October 1966, and a new set of Bye-Laws was drawn up and accepted in due course. The Mission thus adopted the new Constitution, many years after the formation of the Council in 1921, to strengthen the life of the Spreading Tree in accordance with the growing needs and wider challenges of the present time.

The General Council first met in London on May 1st and 2nd, 1967, with 21 elected members present, 15 representatives of Auxiliaries, 5 members of Headquarters staff, and a number of visitors, including several missionaries home on furlough. Sir Harry Greenfield, C.S.I., C.I.E., was elected Chairman of the new General Council, and Sir Paul Benthall, K.B.E., Honorary Treasurer of the Mission. The Council heard reports from all the fields and the Auxiliaries, and from the various Headquarters departments—promotional, editorial, financial, recruitment of missionaries, and so on.

The meeting of the General Council thus provided an opportunity of considering in broad outline (detail being left to the monthly meetings of the Executive Committee) the whole enterprise in which the Mission is engaged.

To gather together in one series the conference of National Secretaries at Hildenborough Hall, the meeting of the General Council itself, the Annual Meeting of Members of the Mission, and the Annual Public Meeting of the Society, had obvious advantages, apart from the saving in travel costs. The new arrangement also made quite heavy demands on the staff at Headquarters, and on the members of the Executive Committee, who, instead of meeting two or three times a year as occasion required, were now asked to meet monthly—a real sacrifice of time by busy and important people.

One item of business on which we must comment occupied for a time a somewhat lowly place in the agenda of the General Council, and then suddenly in 1970 its importance was such that it came first in the long list of reports. The subject was finance, and if any members of the General Council were unaware of the situation, Torrie Attwell must have given them a shock, for he announced that for the first time in very many years the accounts for 1969 had shown a large deficit, and it had been necessary to draw over £39,000 from reserves to balance the accounts. This deficit was not due to a big drop in income. There had in fact been a reduction in the contributions from American Leprosy Missions, some of their grants being sent direct to the field and not through London, but this was offset by increases in the amounts raised by several Auxiliaries. There were two main causes—the general rise in costs and the rapidly expanding out-patient work. So even though in 1969 total ordinary income amounted to the magnificent sum of £458,500, and income from legacies reached a new record total of £154,760, total expenditure had also shown an increase of £45,000 on the previous year, thus putting the accounts in serious deficit for 1969.

Although this may have come as a shock to some members of the General Council and to many readers of *An Open Door*, the Mission's Annual Report for 1969, there had in fact been warnings of the approaching crisis.

Dr. Victor Das in 1968 had indicated one main cause of the deficit, which was the increasing number of patients attending clinics, coupled with the rise in the cost of maintaining in-patients in institutions. It seemed that the Mission could not go on carrying these two burdens at the same time. He recommended that the Mission's policy should now be to reduce the number of in-patients and reach out into surrounding areas, wherever possible at little extra cost. This suggestion was followed up.

In the meantime, Dr. Paul Brand had made a study of the cost-effectiveness of leprosy work. He found that the cost of maintaining a patient in hospital was about 150 units per annum, while that of treating an out-patient was only 15 units, just one tenth of the former figure. To go out to sufferers from leprosy in their villages was therefore much cheaper than to admit them to hospital. Was this therefore a better use of the Mission's resources?

The scientific and professional view would appear to be that it was, but other considerations might weigh against this, such as the need for spiritual ministry along with the prevention and healing. The outreach of the Spreading Tree to great numbers of people offered wide opportunities for evangelism, for at every clinic the word of the Gospel may be proclaimed, but in such circumstances the pastoral ministry which had been such a fruitful agency of Christian compassion in the Mission's Homes, often carried on for years, obviously could not be so easily exercised.

Clearly there is a big question here concerning the ratio of in-patient to out-patient work involving stewardship of the Lord's money entrusted to the Mission by His people.

The financial situation improved somewhat in 1970 and a deficit was avoided. The response from the Auxiliaries was an excellent one, the total for ordinary income standing at the high figure of £469,300, excluding grants and gifts received and expended on the field with several Auxiliaries showing substantial increases.

During the period 1965 to 1970 Mr. Newberry Fox's policy for Europe was energetically implemented and in 1966 the Rev. Dr. P. C. Toureille, whom we have already met at Valbonne, was appointed Secretary for Europe. Progress was soon evident in Switzerland, France, and Germany, where a Committee was formed and held its first meeting, attended by the Financial Secretary of the Mission, in 1967, and contacts were reported in Italy, Spain, Belgium, Holland, Finland, Norway, and even Czechoslovakia, while at least one substantial contribution was received from Austria. Also in 1967 the European Leprosy Association, known as E.L.E.P., which are the initials of its Continental title, was formed, and The Leprosy Mission became a member.

Interest in leprosy in Europe was further stimulated by the meeting of the International Congress of Leprology in London in September 1969, when over 500 doctors and others interested in leprosy, from 70 different countries, spent six days in asking and answering questions about leprosy from almost every imaginable point of view. Dr. Stanley G. Browne was the leader of a strong Mission delegation at this Congress, and was warmly congratulated by the Council on the excellent arrangements he and his staff had made for it. Here are two comments on the Congress from Dr. Browne:

> The acknowledged leader of a fine research team in the U.S.A. gave out his opinion that 'thanks to the London Congress, the science of leprosy has now arrived'. Somebody else, a layman, equally eminent in his own field, and of course not competent to comment on scientific achievements, thought that never had so much interest been shown at such a Congress in the patient as a person needing a sympathetic approach and medically competent help.

By 1970 the work in Europe had reached the point where Dr. Toureille needed help, and the Rev. Henry Aalto, of Finland, was appointed to assist him.

In 1967 Denmark celebrated the 25th anniversary of the establishment of the Auxiliary in 1947. Miss Anna Wiesel had been obliged to retire from the Secretaryship of the Auxiliary earlier in the year on account of ill-health; she had given twenty years of service to the cause and had seen the income of the Danish Auxiliary rise from £600 in 1950 to £16,000 in 1967.

The Rev. C. M. Lloyd became Secretary for England and Wales at the end of 1967, thus adding another chapter to his varied experience in Burma, Korea, and India.

In New Zealand, the Rev, Murray H. Feist retired in 1968, and was succeeded by the Rev. R. A. Alcorn. Mr. Alcorn entered upon a great tradition of dynamic leadership, for during Mr. Feist's Secretaryship the income of the Auxiliary had risen from £18,665 in 1950 to £145,590 in 1961! The award of the M.B.E. to Mr. Feist in 1970 was a fitting recognition of a remarkable record of service.

In 1969 the Rev. H. D. Graham, M.A., of Glasgow, was offered and accepted the Secretaryship of the Canadian Auxiliary.

During the five years now being reviewed relations with American Leprosy Missions changed somewhat, as policies tended to diverge from the close partnership achieved in 1963. The American Society decided to withdraw its support from the Leprosy Study Centre in London, though Dr. Hasselblad was asked to retain his membership of the Committee. Similarly there was renewed discussion of the principle of the co-operative budget. It seems that friends in America, like the leaders of the Mission in Great Britain, were making a reappraisal of the most effective ways of using available resources in a rapidly developing concept of what leprosy work now means.

At Headquarters Dr. Neil Fraser, as already mentioned, retired as Medical Secretary in 1966 and he and his wife went to live in Pitlochry in Perthshire, which Dr. Fraser used as a base for the valuable help he was able to give to the Scottish Auxiliary. But not for long. On August 3rd, 1969 he came to the end of his service for the suffering, having fought a good fight and finished his course. His obituary in the Mission magazine was appropriately entitled 'Passing of a Pioneer' and gave an account of his long career:

> His leprosy work began when he was appointed to Swatow, S.W. China, in 1924, as a medical missionary of the English Presbyterian Mission. Later he served in Swabue and Wukingfu and, after the withdrawal of the Society from China, the Overseas Missionary Council lent him to The Mission to Lepers as Secretary for China and Hong Kong. In this capacity Dr. Fraser accepted responsibility for the founding of the Isle of Happy Healing (Hay Ling Chau), Hong Kong. He saw the work develop from a barren island to a modern centre of leprosy care and rehabilitation which has gained a world reputation. At the request of Council, Dr. Fraser joined the London Headquarters staff in 1960 to become Medical Secretary, a post which took him on many extensive tours of investigation and demonstration. His period as Medical Secretary was marked by advances in medicine, surgery, and rehabilitation, and his long experience and accumulated knowledge, especially in clinical aspects of the disease, led to requests for help from many Mission and Government institutions.

Hong Kong had special reason to remember Dr. Fraser and there has been erected to his memory the beautiful Fraser Memorial Gate on the Island to which he gave so much.

The Most Rev. George O. Simms, Ph.D., D.D., Archbishop of Dublin and Primate of All Ireland, consented to fill the vacancy caused by the resignation of Lord Fisher of Lambeth, and accepted election to the Presidency of the Mission, thus restoring that close link with Dublin and the Church of Ireland which had been so great a source of strength in former years.

On June 17th, 1970 the Council gave a party to celebrate the ninetieth birthday of that great veteran of the anti-leprosy campaign, Dr. Ernest Muir, C.M.G., C.I.E., M.D., F.R.C.S., LL.D., when many friends gathered to wish him well and to exchange reminiscences as incidents in his long career were recalled by several speakers. Among the outstanding events of 1970 were the dedication of the new Headquarters of the Mission at 50, Portland Place, London, W.1., by the President of the Mission on February 20th; and the formal opening of the new office on May 1st by Lady Templer, the wife of Field Marshal Sir Gerald Templer, Lord Lieutenant of Greater London, before a large company. Sir Harry Greenfield, who presided on this important occasion, quoted most aptly words used by Mr. Wellesley Bailey in 1917 at the opening of the Mission's first real headquarters in Dublin:

> I pray for this place where we shall meet God face to face, where we shall hear His voice and feel His guidance and learn His will. I feel very keenly today that so much depends upon a continual waiting upon God. The living prayer of Christian people is that we should be led and guided by prayer. I pray God that His abundant blessing may be poured out upon this work in the days to come as it has been in the past.

Sir Harry continued:

> Now to that eloquent and echoing invocation by our Founder I suggest that the answer of all of us here today must be a devout 'Amen'.

So it came about that a few days later the General Council of 1970 met for the first time on the Mission's own premises, though the Annual Public Meeting was held as usual at Caxton Hall. Members of the Council were unanimous in praise of the facilities now provided at 50 Portland Place.

As the new property is held on a very long lease it may now be regarded as the Mission's permanent home. So it is appropriate that this part of the Mission's long history should come to a close at this point.

So far this chapter has been concerned with constitutional and organizational matters of importance in the story of the Spreading Tree. But it seems right to recall at this point the individual patient and what happened to him or her, and for this last story of this kind we are indebted to Miss M. W. J. Evans, who published in the 1968 issue of the magazine an account of the new work in Calcutta to which she had felt led. Actually this centre of Christian work was not established in Calcutta itself, but in the twin city of Howrah on the other side of the River Hoogly, joined to Calcutta by the magnificent span of the famous Howrah Bridge.

The new bridge, built during World War II, is a cantilever bridge, a great single span of silvery steel over which moves a constant flow of noisy traffic; crowded buses, aggressive taxis, rickshaws, bicycles, carts drawn by people and by patient buffaloes, hand trolleys and people; always people, thousands of them, because the population of Calcutta and Howrah, now more than four-and-a-half million, is growing continually, and overcrowding is a chronic problem. Thousands of people know no other home than the pavements. Tens of thousands live in crowded slums and, on the Howrah side, within view of the new bridge, small tumbledown houses jostle each other for breathing space. There is tremendous need in Howrah: hunger, poverty, and sickness, but life goes on and it is here, in this area of need, that a new centre of Christian witness has begun, an outreach of compassion to the deprived.

After her long and distinguished service at Purulia, Miss Joan Evans now set about her task in this another area of great need. And who were her helpers? Two of them were ex-patients whom Miss Evans had known for some time at the Purulia Home.

Surobhita was a farmer's daughter, a low-caste Hindu who came to the Purulia Leprosy Home as a teenager, greatly distressed when her family realized that she had leprosy. While she took treatment in the leprosy hospital, she went to school. With an effort she learned to read and write and was later trained to do simple nursing work in the hospital wards. The way in which she was cared for worked on her heart and mind, and one day Surobhita asked to be baptized. In 1957 the doctors pronounced her free from leprosy and she went home happily, nearly twenty years after admission.

The joy of family reunion was great, but it did not last; the neighbours in the village saw to that. They objected to her return because of her old disease and because she had become a Christian. The family were not allowed to use the communal well, and eventually Surobhita was forced to leave home again. She went to a bigger village near Purulia, and lived on charity, often travelling as far as Calcutta, 200 miles away, seeking alms. She hated the life and was overjoyed when Miss Evans offered her work, first in the garden and then later, working as a house servant. A room was found for her, away from the beggar village, and life opened up again for Surobhita. She is a good worker and a good listener to people in need. The heartaches of her own life have given her a lively sympathy for others, and her Christian faith has made her ready to help. So God prepared the life of a simple Bengali Christian for a part in His plans for Howrah.

The other helper had a quite different background because she came from a different social order.

Chameli was a high-caste woman, married, living in Calcutta. Leprosy does not recognize social status, and Chameli had to go to Purulia for reconstructive surgery to remedy the damage it had caused to her hands and feet. Whilst in hospital, there were complications to Chameli's family life. Her husband disappeared with their small son. Her letters to them were returned 'Not known, gone away'. In 1962 Chameli too accepted Christ. She worked in the hospital and taught in the adult literacy classes. Three years later her husband turned up and there was a short-lived reconciliation, but pressure from the husband's relatives was relentless. Chameli was partially disabled and was thus an embarrassment to them. She was also a Christian, and they insisted that she renounce her faith or leave. She left, and after another period of treatment in Purulia for foot complications she was ready for discharge when the time came for the first moves in this new project in Howrah.

All honour to these two who had passed through deep waters of suffering and sorrow themselves, and therefore had this 'lively sympathy for others', as Miss Evans says, as they turned to help their sisters in poverty and need.

This is our last look at the individual patient. What of the patients in the mass as they came in their crowds to accept the ministry which the Mission was offering to them in the name of Christ? At the end of 1970 what was the full extent of the Spreading Tree?

The answer is found in two sentences, taken from the leaflet advertising the Annual Public Meeting of 1971, all the more striking by reason of the very brevity of the statement:

> The Mission works among 250,000 patients at 188 centres in 34 countries either in its own leprosy homes, hospitals or out-patient clinics, or in co-operation with other Christian Societies or Churches. Nearly 90 Missionary Societies and national Churches receive help from The Leprosy Mission as part of its programme for aid to leprosy sufferers.

If Wellesley Bailey had been with us today, what would he have said to that? Surely he would have been amazed at the wonderful growth of the Spreading Tree from its modest beginnings, and he would surely have given thanks to God for this astonishing increase through the years. Equally surely he would now call upon us to do the same and offer our thanksgiving to God in Christ, for it is His power that has made fruitful the ministry of His servants, His grace that has crowned their faithfulness with success, His lovingkindness that has blessed us all, both those who have been privileged to serve and those to whom the service was offered so that they might receive new life and hope through His redemptive love.

Now to Him who has brought us to this day with His praise on our lips,
Who will also surely lead us in the coming days into a fuller knowledge of His will for us,
TO THE ONLY WISE GOD OUR SAVIOUR, BE GLORY AND MAJESTY, DOMINION AND POWER, BOTH NOW AND EVER. AMEN.

THE LEPROSY MISSION

AUSTRALIA, 174 Collins Street, Melbourne, Vic, 3000; CANADA, Suite 1128, 67 Yonge Street, Toronto, Ont.; ENGLAND AND WALES, 50 Portland Place, London W1N 3DG; HONG KONG, P.O. Box 380, Hong Kong; INDIA, 5 Ratendon Road, New Delhi, 110003; IRELAND, 20 Lincoln Place, Dublin 2; NORTH OF IRELAND, 44 Ulsterville Avenue, Belfast BT9 7AQ; NEW ZEALAND, 43-45 Mount Eden Road, Auckland 3; SCOTLAND, 11 Coates Crescent, Edinburgh EH3 7AL; SOUTHERN AFRICA, 30 Seventh Avenue, Highlands North, Johannesburg; EUROPE, 6 Rue des Fossés, 1110 Morges (Vaud), Switzerland; SCANDINAVIA, Hakolahdentie 10 A 9, SF-00200 Helsinki 20, Finland; BELGIUM, Rue Julien d'Andrimont 7, 4000 Liege; DENMARK, Lundevej 19, Horsholm; FRANCE, 15 Rue Grignan, 13006 Marseille; GERMANY, 821 Prien am Chiemsee, Am Berg 8; ITALY, Ghigo 10060 Prali (To); SPAIN, Bravo Murillo 85, Madrid 3; SWEDEN, Valtvagen II, 17544 Jarfalla; and SWITZERLAND, 4622 Egerkingen, Postfach 22.